MW00973981

SRA ART Connections

Level K

Authors

Rosalind Ragans, Ph.D., Senior Author

Willis "Bing" Davis   Jane Rhoades Hudak, Ph.D.   Bunyan Morris
Tina Farrell   Gloria McCoy   Nan Yoshida

Contributing Author

Jackie Ellett

ART
SOU
RCE
ARTSOURCE

Education Division
The Music Center of Los Angeles County

Columbus, OH

The McGraw·Hill Companies

Authors

Senior Author
Dr. Rosalind Ragans, Ph.D.
Associate Professor Emerita
Georgia Southern University

Willis "Bing" Davis
Associate Professor Emeritus
Central State University - Ohio
President & Founder of
SHANGO: The Center for the
Study of African American
Art & Culture

Tina Farrell
Assistant Superintendent
Curriculum and Instruction
Clear Creek Independent
School District,
League City, Texas

Jane Rhoades Hudak, Ph.D.
Professor of Art
Georgia Southern University

Gloria McCoy
Former President
Texas Art Education Association
Spring Branch Independent
School District, Texas

Bunyan Morris
Art Teacher
Effingham County School
System, Springfield, Georgia

Nan Yoshida
Art Education Consultant
Retired Art Supervisor
Los Angeles Unified
School District
Los Angeles, California

SRAonline.com

SRA

Send all inquiries to:
SRA/McGraw-Hill
8787 Orion Place
Columbus, OH 43240-4027

Printed in the United States of America.

ISBN 0-07-601819-9

1 2 3 4 5 6 7 8 9 RRW 10 09 08 07 06 05 04

Contributors

Contributing Author
Jackie Ellett
Elementary Art Teacher
Duncan Creek Elementary School
Hoschton, Georgia

Artsource® Music, Dance, Theatre Lessons
Mark Slavkin, Vice President
for Education, The Music Center of
Los Angeles County
Michael Solomon, Managing Director
Music Center Education Division
Melinda Williams, Concept Originator and
Project Director
Susan Cambigue-Tracey, Project Coordinator
and Writer
Madeleine Dahm, Movement and Dance
Connection Writer
Keith Wyffels, Staff Assistance
Maureen Erbe, Logo Design

More about Aesthetics
Richard W. Burrows
Executive Director, Institute for Arts
Education
San Diego, California

Safe Use of Art Materials
Mary Ann Boykin
Director, The Art School for Children and
Young Adults
University of Houston—Clear Lake
Houston, Texas

Museum Education
Marilyn J. S. Goodman
Director of Education
Solomon R. Guggenheim Museum
New York, New York

Resources for Students with Disabilities
Mandy Yeager
Ph.D. Candidate
The University of North Texas
Denton, Texas

Music Connections
Kathy Mitchell
Music Teacher
Eagan, Minnesota

Student Activities

Cassie Appleby
Glen Oaks Elementary School
McKinney, Texas

Maureen Banks
Kester Magnet School
Van Nuys, California

Christina Barnes
Webb Bridge Middle School
Alpharetta, Georgia

Beth Benning
Willis Jepson Middle School
Vacaville, California

Chad Buice
Craig Elementary School
Snellville, Georgia

Beverly Broughton
Gwinn Oaks Elementary School
Snellville, Georgia

Missy Burgess
Jefferson Elementary School
Jefferson, Georgia

Marcy Cincotta-Smith
Benefield Elementary School
Lawrenceville, Georgia

Joanne Cox
Kittredge Magnet School
Atlanta, Georgia

Carolyn Y. Craine
McCracken County Schools
Mayfield, Kentucky

Jackie Ellett
Duncan Creek Elementary School
Hoschton, Georgia

Tracie Flynn
Home School
Rushville, Indiana

Phyllis Glenn
Malcom Bridge Elementary
Bogart, Georgia

Dallas Gillespie
Dacula Middle School
Dacula, Georgia

Dr. Donald Gruber
Clinton Junior High School
Clinton, Illinois

Karen Heid
Rock Springs Elementary School
Lawrenceville, Georgia

Alisa Hyde
Southwest Elementary
Savannah, Georgia

Kie Johnson
Oconee Primary School
Watkinsville, Georgia

Sallie Keith, NBCT
West Side Magnet School
LaGrange, Georgia

Letha Kelly
Grayson Elementary School
Grayson, Georgia

Diane Kimiera
Amestoy Elementary School
Gardena, California

Desiree LaOrange
Barkley Elementary School
Fort Campbell, Kentucky

Deborah Lackey-Wilson
Roswell North Elementary
Roswell, Georgia

Dawn Laird
Goforth Elementary School
Clear Creek, Texas

Mary Lazzari
Timothy Road Elementary School
Athens, Georgia

Michelle Leonard
Webb Bridge Middle School
Alpharetta, Georgia

Lynn Ludlam
Spring Branch ISD
Houston, Texas

Mark Mitchell
Fort Daniel Elementary School
Dacula, Georgia

Martha Moore
Freeman's Mill Elementary School
Dacula, Georgia

Connie Niedenthal
Rushville Elementary
Rushville, Indiana

Barbara Patisaul
Oconee County Elementary
School
Watkinsville, Georgia

Elizabeth Paulos-Krasle
Social Circle Elementary
Social Circle, Georgia

Jane Pinneau
Rocky Branch Elementary School
Watkinsville, Georgia

Marilyn Polin
Cutler Ridge Middle School
Miami, Florida

Michael Ramsey
Graves County Schools
Paducah, Kentucky

Rosemarie Sells
Social Circle Elementary
Social Circle, Georgia

Jean Neelen Siegel
Baldwin School
California

Debra Smith
McIntosh County School System
Darien, Georgia

Patricia Spencer
Harmony Elementary School
Buford, Georgia

Melanie Stokes
Smiley Elementary School
Ludowici, Georgia

Rosanne Stutts
Davidson Fine Arts School
Augusta, Georgia

Fran Sullivan
South Jackson Elementary School
Athens, Georgia

Kathy Valentine
Home School
Burkburnett, Texas

Debi West
Rock Springs Elementary School
Lawrenceville, Georgia

Sherry White
Bauerschlog Elementary School
League City, Texas

Patricia Wiesen
Cutler Ridge Middle School
Miami, Florida

Deayna Woodruff
Loveland Middle School
Loveland, Ohio

Gil Young
Beverly Hills Middle School
Beverly Hills, California

Larry A. Young
Dacula Elementary School
Dacula, Georgia

Table of Contents

▲ **Katsushika Hokusai.** *The Great Wave Off Kanagawa.*

Unit 1 Line

◄ **Grant Wood.**
American Gothic.

Unit 2 Shape

◀ **Henri Matisse.**
*Woman in a
Purple Coat.*

Unit 3 Color

◀ **Allan Houser.**
Earth Song.

Unit 4 Space and Form

Unit 5 Texture

▲ **Maria Martinez.** *Two Black-on-Black Pots.*

Unit 6 Principles of Art

Technique Tips

Activity Tips

What Is Art?

Art is . . .

Painting

▲ **Georgia O'Keeffe.** (American). *Autumn Leaves—Lake George.* 1924.
....
Oil on canvas. Columbus Museum of Art, Columbus, Ohio.

Drawing

▲ **Leonardo da Vinci.** (Italian). *Self Portrait.* 1514.
....
Red chalk, Royal Library, Turin, Italy.

Sculpture

▲ **Artist Unknown.** (Italy). *Camillus.* A.D. 41–54.
....
Bronze. $46\frac{7}{8}$ inches high (119.08 cm.). The Metropolitan Museum of Art, New York, New York.

Architecture

▲ **Artist Unknown.** (India). *Taj Mahal.* 1638–1648.
....
Marble. 240 feet tall (73.15 meters). Agra, India.

Printmaking

▲ **Katsushika Hokusai.** (Japanese). *Kirifuri Waterfall on Mt. Kurokami in Shimotsuke Province.* c. 1833–1834.

Color woodblock print. $15\frac{5}{16} \times 10\frac{3}{8}$ inches (38.9 × 26.3 cm.). Honolulu Academy of Arts, Honolulu, Hawaii.

Pottery

▲ **Harrison Mc Intosh.** (American). *Stoneware Vase #661.* 1966.

Glazed stoneware. $15\frac{1}{4} \times 13$ inches (38.74 × 33.02 cm.). Renwick Gallery, Smithsonian American Art Museum, Washington, D.C.

Weaving

▲ **Artist Unknown.** (Ashanti Peoples, Ghana). *Kente Cloth.*

Museum of International Folk Art, Santa Fe, New Mexico.

Clothing

◀ **Artist Unknown.** (American). *Arapaho Man's Shirt.* c. 1890.

Buckskin and feathers. 37 inches (93.68 cm.) long. Buffalo Bill Historical Center, Cody, Wyoming.

Art is created by people.

What Is Art?

Every work of art has three parts.

Subject

This is the object you see in the artwork.

Composition

This is how the artwork is organized.

Content

This is what the artwork means.

▲ **W.H. Brown.** (American). *Bareback Riders.* 1886.

Oil on cardboard mounted on wood. $18\frac{1}{2} \times 24\frac{1}{2}$ inches (46.99 × 61.60 cm.). National Gallery of Art, Washington, D.C.

What is the subject of this artwork?

▲ **Artist Unknown.** (Native American, Navajo). *Classic Serape Style Wearing Blanket.* 1875.

Plied cotton and Saxony wool. $73\frac{1}{2} \times 47$ inches (186.69 × 119.38 cm.). Utah Museum of Fine Arts, University of Utah, Salt Lake City, Utah.

How is this work organized?

▲ **Jacob Lawrence.** (American). *Children at Play.* 1947.

Tempera on Masonite panel. 20 × 24 inches (50.8 × 60.96 cm.). Georgia Museum of Art, University of Georgia, Athens, Georgia.

What does this artwork mean?

What Is Art?

Subject Matter

Artists make art about many subjects. Name the subjects you see on these pages.

Colors and Shapes

▲ **Auguste Herbin.** (French). *Composition on the Word "Vie" 2.*
1950.

Oil on canvas. $57\frac{1}{2} \times 38\frac{1}{4}$ inches (146.05 × 97.16 cm.). Museum of Modern Art, New York, New York.

Things Outside

▲ **Claude Monet.** (French). *The Four Trees.* 1891.
Oil on canvas. $32\frac{1}{4} \times 32\frac{1}{8}$ inches (81.92×81.58 cm.). The Metropolitan Museum of Art, New York, New York.

What Is Art?

Everyday Life

▲ **Carmen Lomas Garza.** (American). *Naranjas (Oranges).*

Gouache. 20 × 14 inches (50.8 × 35.56 cm.). Collection of Mr. and Mrs. Ira Schneider, Scottsdale, Arizona.

A Story

▲ **Artist Unknown.** (Hmong Peoples, Asia). *Hmong Story Cloth.*

Cotton. 18 × 18 inches (45.72 × 45.72 cm.). Private collection.

What Is Art?

People

▲ **Isabel Bishop.** (American). *Ice Cream Cones.* 1942.
. . . .
Oil and egg tempera on fiberboard. $33\frac{7}{8}$ x 20 inches (86.04 x 50.8 cm.).
Museum of Fine Arts, Boston, Massachusetts.

Objects

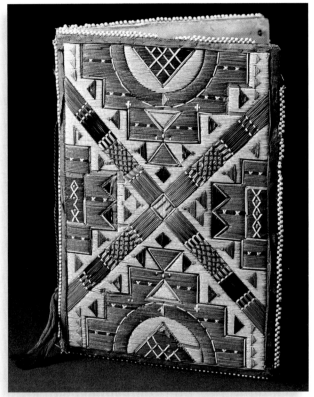

▲ **Artist Unknown.** (Mi'kmaq People, Nova Scotia, Canada). *Letter Holder or Book Cover.*

Birch bark decorated with porcupine quills, glass beads, and silk. $10\frac{1}{4} \times 14\frac{1}{2}$ inches (26.04 × 36.83 cm.). Museum of International Folk Art, Santa Fe, New Mexico.

Things with a Deeper Meaning

▲ **Rufino Tamayo.** (Mexican). *Toast to the Sun.* 1956.

Oil on canvas. $31\frac{1}{2}$ x 39 inches (80 x 99 cm.). Wichita Art Museum, Wichita, Kansas.

What Is Art?

Elements of Art

Art talks with . . .

Line

Shape

Form

Space

Color

Value

Texture

Principles of Art

Pattern

Rhythm

Balance

Emphasis

Harmony

Variety

Unity

▲ **Mary Cassatt.** (American). *Susan Comforting the Baby.* 1881.

Oil on canvas. 25$\frac{5}{8}$ x 39$\frac{3}{8}$ inches (65.1 x 100 cm.). Museum of Fine Arts, Houston, Texas.

Art History and Culture

Look at the painting.

▶ How are the people dressed?

▶ What are they doing?

▶ What can you learn about the artist?

About Art

▲ **Mary Cassatt.** (American). *Susan Comforting the Baby.* 1881.

Oil on canvas. $25\frac{5}{8}$ x $39\frac{3}{8}$ inches (65.1 x 100 cm.). Museum of Fine Arts, Houston, Texas.

Aesthetic Perception

Look

▶ Look at the work of art.
What do you see?

Look Inside

▶ Pretend you are Susan.
Tell a story about this work of art.

Look Outside

▶ How does this work make you feel?

▶ What will you remember about this
work of art?

About Art

▲ **Mary Cassatt.** (American). *Susan Comforting the Baby.* 1881.
· ·
Oil on canvas. $25\frac{5}{8}$ x $39\frac{3}{8}$ inches (65.1 x 100 cm.). Museum of Fine Arts, Houston, Texas.

Art Criticism

Describe

▶ List the people and things you see.

Analyze

▶ What lines, shapes, colors, and textures do you see?

▶ What part stands out?

Interpret

▶ What is happening? What is the artist telling you about Susan and the baby?

Decide

▶ Have you ever seen another artwork like this?

About Art

▲ **Mary Cassatt.** (American). *Susan Comforting the Baby.* 1881.
Oil on canvas. $25\frac{5}{8}$ x $39\frac{3}{8}$ inches (65.1 x 100 cm.). Museum of Fine Arts, Houston, Texas.

Creative Expression

How can you make art?

1. Get an idea.
2. Plan your work.
3. Make a sketch.
4. Use the media.
5. Share your final work.

Safety

▶ Use art materials only on your artwork.

▶ Keep art materials out of your mouth, eyes, and ears.

▶ Use only safety scissors. Keep your fingers away from the blades.

► Wash your hands after using the art materials.

► Wear an art shirt or smock to protect your clothes.

► Always follow your teacher's directions.

Line

Artists use lines to create their works of art.

▲ **Katsushika Hokusai.**
(Japanese). *The Great Wave Off Kanagawa.* 1831–1833.

Polychrome woodblock print. $10\frac{1}{8} \times 14\frac{15}{16}$
inches (25.72 × 37.95 cm.).
The Metropolitan Museum of Art,
New York, New York.

Artists use many types of lines.

► Can you find some different kinds of lines?

In This Unit you will:

► learn about lines.

► see how artists use lines to make their works of art.

► use lines in your artwork.

Self-Portrait.

Katsushika Hokusai
(1760–1849)

Katsushika Hokusai

► was a Japanese artist.

► created prints.

► made landscapes.

Lesson 1 Thick and Thin Lines

Look at the Native American blankets. The artists used thick and thin lines in their blankets.

◄ **Artist Unknown.** (Native American, Navajo). *Classic Serape Style Wearing Blanket.* 1875.

Plied cotton and Saxony wool. $73\frac{1}{2} \times 47$ inches (186.69 × 119.38 cm.). Utah Museum of Fine Arts, University of Utah, Salt Lake City, Utah.

 Art History and Culture

Native American artists get ideas from nature. What things have you seen in nature that look like the lines on the blankets?

▲ **Sylvia Long.** (American).
Illustration from *Ten Little Rabbits*,
by Virginia Grossman. ©1991.

Pen, ink, and watercolor. Chronicle Books,
San Francisco, California.

Study both works of art.

▶ Where do you see thick lines?

▶ Where do you see thin lines?

 **Aesthetic Perception**

Design Awareness Find thick and thin lines on
the walls and floor of the classroom.

Using Thick and Thin Lines

A **thick line** is wide.

A **thin line** is narrow.

Practice

1. Stand and line up with some classmates. Form a thin line.
2. Next form a thick line with your classmates.

 Kristina Jimenez.
Age 5.

Think about the kinds of lines you see in the student's artwork.

 **Creative Expression**

How would you use thick and thin lines to make a design?

1. Think about thick and thin lines.

2. Create a blanket for yourself with different lines.

Art Criticism

Describe How many thick lines did you paint? Thin lines?

2 Lines Can Make Calm Pictures

◀ **Claude Monet.**
(French). *The Four Trees.* 1891.
. . . .
Oil on canvas. $32\frac{1}{4} \times 32\frac{1}{8}$ inches (81.92 × 81.58 cm.). The Metropolitan Museum of Art, New York, New York.

Look at these works of art. Artists use **vertical** and **horizontal lines** to make art look calm.

 Art History and Culture

Some artists, such as Monet, like to paint outside. They show how the natural light looks in their paintings.

▲ **David Hockney.** (British). *American Collectors.* 1968.

Acrylic on canvas. $63\frac{7}{8} \times 120$ inches (213.4 × 304.8 cm.). The Art Institute of Chicago, Chicago, Illinois.

Study both works of art.

▶ Where do you see vertical lines?

▶ Where do you see horizontal lines?

Aesthetic Perception

Seeing Like an Artist Where do you see vertical and horizontal lines outside?

Using Vertical and Horizontal Lines

Vertical lines move up and down.

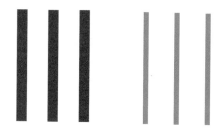

Horizontal lines move from side to side.

Practice

1. Use your finger to draw a vertical line in the air.

2. Now draw a horizontal line in the air.

◄ **Thomas Lazzari.**
Age 5.

Think about where vertical and horizontal lines are used in this student's work.

 **Creative Expression**

How can you make a picture look calm?

1. Tear the paper into short and long pieces.
2. Place the pieces on the page to make a calm landscape.
3. Glue the pieces to the page.

 **Art Criticism**

Interpret What appears to be standing still in your picture?

Lesson 3 Lines Can Make Busy Pictures

▲ **W. H. Brown.** (American).
Bareback Riders. 1886.
....
Oil on cardboard mounted on wood.
$18\frac{1}{2} \times 24\frac{1}{4}$ inches (46.99 × 61.60 cm.).
National Gallery of Art, Washington, D.C.

Look at the artwork on these pages. Both works of art look busy.

 Art History and Culture

Artists create art for many reasons. The artist made *Humpty Dumpty Circus* so it could be used as a toy.

▲ *Schoenhut's*
Humpty Dumpty Circus.

Toy Sculpture. Children's Museum of
Indianapolis, Indiana.

Study both pictures.

▶ Where are diagonal lines?

▶ Where are zigzag lines?

Aesthetic Perception

Seeing Like an Artist Can you find diagonal
and zigzag lines around you?

Using Diagonal and Zigzag Lines

Lines move in different directions.

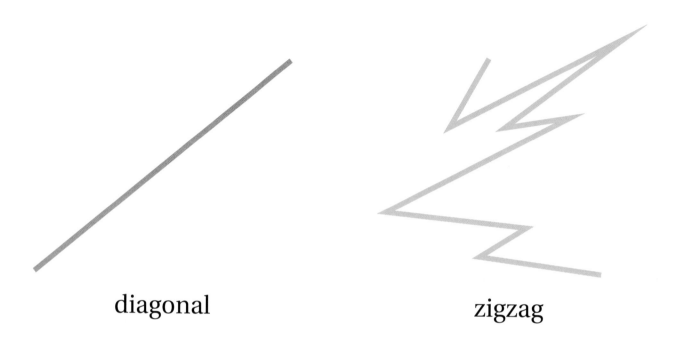

diagonal

zigzag

Practice

1. Pretend you are a circus performer.

2. Ask classmates to guess what you are doing.

Think about how this artist used diagonal and zigzag lines.

◄ **Grayson Hulett.**
Age 5.

 Creative Expression

What lines do you see on a clown?

1. Use the shape and pencil tools to draw a clown.

2. Make the hair by drawing zigzag lines.

3. Decorate the costume with diagonal lines.

 Art Criticism

Decide Can you draw your picture using only diagonal lines?

Curved Lines

◀ **William Blake.** (British). *The Fly* from *Songs of Innocence and of Experience.* c. 1825.

Color-printed relief etching. 6 3/16 in. × 5 9/16 inches (15.7 × 14.1 cm.). The Metropolitan Museum of Art, New York, New York.

Look at the pictures. These artists used curved lines to show things moving.

 Art History and Culture

Sometimes works of art tell a story. What story do you think is being told in each picture?

Study the pictures.

▶ What things look like they are moving?

▶ Where do you see curved lines?

◀ **Katsushika Hokusai.** (Japanese). *Boy Juggling Shells.* Edo period.

Album leaf, ink, and color on paper. $13\frac{5}{16} \times 9\frac{1}{2}$ inches (33.81 × 24.13 cm.). The Metropolitan Museum of Art, New York, New York.

Aesthetic Perception

Seeing Like an Artist Trace in the air one thing that you see in one of the pictures.

Using Curved Lines to Show Movement

Curved lines show things moving.

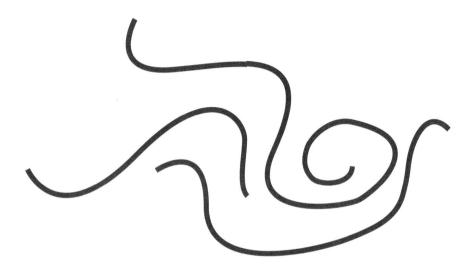

1. Listen as the teacher calls out a movement.

2. Keep making the movement until the teacher says "freeze."

◀ **Tiffany Palmer.**
Age 5.

Think about how this student artist made things look like they are moving.

 **Creative Expression**

How would you show yourself moving in a picture?

1. Think of your favorite game to play on the playground.

2. Draw a picture of yourself playing.

3. Use curved and diagonal lines to show things moving.

 **Art Criticism**

Analyze Name the different kinds of lines you used to create your drawing.

Smooth and Rough Lines

Look at the pictures of the cats. Do you see how the cats look different? Some lines look smooth and some look rough.

▲ **Theophile-Alexandre Steinlen.** (Swiss/French). *L'Hiver: Chat sur un Coussin (Winter: Cat on a Cushion).* 1909.

Color lithograph. 20 × 24 inches (50.8 × 60.96 cm.). The Metropolitan Museum of Art, New York, New York.

 **Art History and Culture**

Steinlen often showed his own cats in his art.

▲ **Currier and Ives.**
(American). *My
Little White Kittens
into Mischief.* 1865.
• • • • • • • • • • • • • • •
Hand-colored lithograph.
$8\frac{1}{4} \times 12\frac{1}{2}$ inches
(20.96 × 31.75 cm.). The
Metropolitan Museum of
Art, New York, New York.

Study both works of art.

▶ Where do you see smooth lines?

▶ Where do you see rough lines?

🔍 **Aesthetic Perception**

Design Awareness Look around the room. Find
something that looks smooth.

Using Smooth and Rough Lines

Lines can make things look **smooth.**

Lines can look **rough.**

Practice

1. Draw a smooth line on your paper.
2. Draw a rough line on your paper.

▲ **Hillary Lawrence.**
Age 5.

Think about where you see smooth and rough lines in this picture.

What kind of pet do you like?

1. Think about different types of pets.

2. Draw a pet using smooth and rough lines.

Analyze Where are the smooth lines? Where are the rough lines?

Lesson 6 · Broken Lines

◄ **Louis Comfort Tiffany.**
(American). *Garden Landscape and Fountain.* c. 1905–1915.

Favrile-glass mosaic, cement. Landscape:
8 feet 7½ inches × 9 feet 6 inches
(2.63 × 2.90 meters). Fountain and base:
24 × 77 × 61¾ inches (60.96 × 195.58 × 156.85 cm.).

Look at both works of art. This type of artwork is called a **mosaic.** Artists use small pieces of glass or stone to make broken lines in mosaics.

 Art History and Culture

Artists have been making mosaics for thousands of years. They are usually made on floors or walls.

▲ **Marc Chagall.** (Russian).
The Four Seasons. 1974.
. . . .
Ceramic mosaic. 70 × 10 × 14 feet
(21.34 × 3.05 × 4.27 meters). First
National Bank Plaza, Chicago, Illinois.

Study both works of art.

▶ Find a broken line.

▶ Trace it with your finger.

🔍 Aesthetic Perception

Seeing Like an Artist Make broken lines with your finger in the air.

Using Broken Lines

Lines with spaces between them are **broken lines.** A mosaic has broken lines. See the spaces between the tiles.

1. Make a solid line with paper clips.

2. Make a broken line with paper clips.

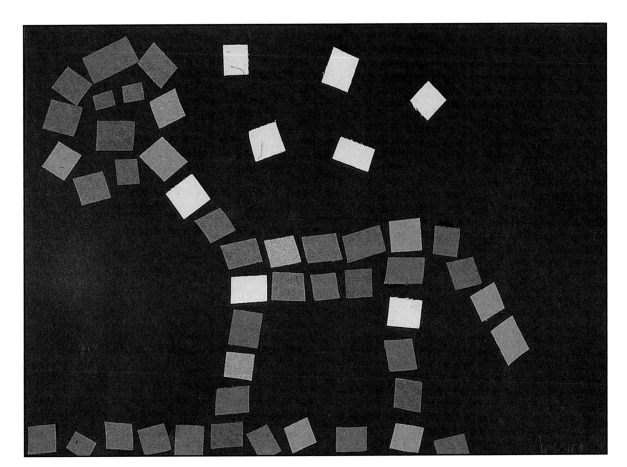

▲ **Jessica M. Hopkins.**
Age 5.

Think about how this student artist used broken lines to make her picture.

How would you make a picture with broken lines?

1. Cut paper strips into small squares.

2. Glue them to the paper to form an outline of an animal.

Decide Do you like the colors you used?

Introduction to Line

▲ **Henri-Charles Manguin.** (French).
Port Saint Tropez, le 14 Juillet. 1905.

Oil on canvas. $24\frac{1}{2} \times 19\frac{3}{4}$ inches (62.23 × 50.17 cm.).
The Museum of Fine Arts, Houston, Houston, Texas.

Describe

▶ Tell what you see in this painting.

Analyze

▶ What kinds of lines do you see in the painting?

Interpret

▶ Do the lines in this painting make it look busy or calm?

Decide

▶ Would you like to see this painting hanging in your school? Why or why not?

Show What You Know

Answer these questions on a sheet of paper.

1 Which of these lines is thick?

A. ────────────

B. �

2 Which of these lines looks calm?

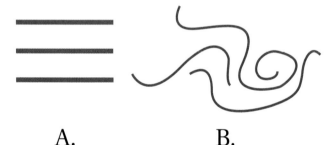

A.   B.

3 Which of these lines is broken?

A. ━━━━━━━━━

B. ─ ─ ─ ─ ─ ─ ─ ─

LET'S VISIT A MUSEUM
The Museum of Fine Arts, Houston

This museum is in Houston, Texas. It is the largest art museum in the Southwest.

Lines in Dance

▲ **Lewitzky Dance Company.**
   "Impressions #2"

Bella Lewitzky creates dances. Her dancers make curved, straight, and slanted lines with their bodies.

What to Do Make lines with your body.

1. Look at the painting. Name the kinds of lines you see.

2. Move your body to show each kind of line.

Art Criticism

Describe What lines did you show with your body?

▲ **Vincent van Gogh.** (Dutch)
The Starry Night. 1889.
....
Oil on canvas. $28\frac{3}{4} \times 36\frac{1}{2}$ inches (73.03 × 92.71 cm.).
Museum of Modern Art. New York, New York.

Shape

Artists use many kinds of shapes in their artwork.

▲ **Grant Wood.** (American). *American Gothic.* 1930.

Oil on beaverboard. $29\frac{1}{4} \times 24\frac{1}{2}$ inches (74.3 × 62.4 cm.). The Art Institute of Chicago, Chicago, Illinois.

Artists use big **shapes** and small **shapes.**

▶ Use your finger to trace shapes you see in the painting.

▶ How are the shapes different?

In This Unit you will:

▶ learn about shapes.

▶ practice using shapes in your artwork.

Return from Bohemia.

Grant Wood
(1891–1942)

▶ was an American artist.

▶ created paintings of farm people and country scenes.

▲ **Maurice Sendak.**
(American). Scene
from *Where the
Wild Things Are.* 1963.
. . . .
Harper and Row Publishers,
New York, New York.

Look at the works of art on these pages. Artists use **outlines** to help us see the **shape** of objects.

 Art History and Culture

Both of these artists created imaginary creatures. How are they alike and different?

◀ **Mercer Mayer.**
(American). Scene
from *There's a
Nightmare in My
Closet.* 1976.
. . . .
Dial Books for Young
Readers, A Member of
Penguin Group (USA) Inc.,
New York, New York.

Study the pictures.

▶ What shapes do you see in the
pictures?

Aesthetic Perception

Seeing Like an Artist Use your finger to trace
a line around something near you. What shape
did you make?

Using Shape

The line around the edge of a **shape** is the **outline.**

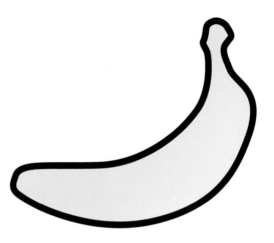

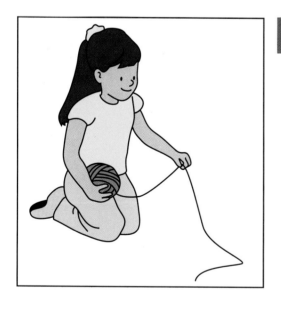

1. Step inside the outline your teacher creates on the floor.

2. Take turns making new shape outlines with the yarn.

Think about the shapes you see in this student's work.

◀ **Seth Paulson.** Age 6.

Creative Expression

What kinds of shapes do imaginary creatures have?

1. Think about the different imaginary creatures you have seen in books.

2. Draw an imaginary creature of your own.

Art Criticism

Interpret Is your picture funny or scary? What makes you think that?

Lesson 2
Geometric Shapes

Look at the shapes in these works of art. They are **geometric shapes.**

◀ **Auguste Herbin.**
(French). *Composition on the Word "Vie" 2.* 1950.

Oil on canvas. $57\frac{1}{2} \times 38\frac{1}{4}$ inches (146.05 × 97.16 cm.). Museum of Modern Art, New York, New York.

 ## Art History and Culture

Some works of art have shapes and designs instead of everyday objects like people or places.

▲ **Wayne Thiebaud.** (American).
Caged Pie. 1962.

Oil on canvas. $20\frac{1}{8} \times 28\frac{1}{8}$ inches
(51.11×71.43 cm.). San Diego Museum
of Art, San Diego, California.

Study the pictures.

▶ Do you know the names of any of
the geometric shapes you see?

Design Awareness Look at your clothes.
Do you see a ■, a ▲, a ●, or a ▬ ?

Using Geometric Shapes

Geometric shapes have names.

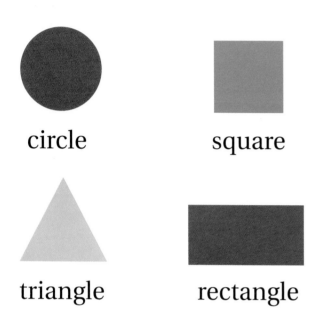

circle

square

triangle

rectangle

Practice

1. Take turns with your partner. Find circles, squares, triangles, and rectangles around you.

2. Draw the shapes you find on your paper. Which shape do you see the most?

Think about the kinds of geometric shapes this student used.

◀ **Jeb Smith.** Age 5.

Creative Expression

What are your favorite geometric shapes?

1. Cut out some shapes.
2. Choose the ones you like best and glue them on the paper.

Art Criticism

Describe How many different geometric shapes did you use? What are the names of the geometric shapes you used?

Free-Form Shapes

▲ **David Wiesner.**
(American). *Free Fall.* 1988.
....
Illustration. Courtesy of Lothrop, Lee, and Shepard Books.

Look at the different shapes in these works of art. Shapes that are not geometric are called **free-form shapes.**

 Art History and Culture

People who draw or paint pictures for books are called illustrators. Their art helps tell stories.

◀ **Georgia O'Keeffe.**
(American). *Autumn Leaves—Lake George.* 1924.

Oil on canvas. Columbus Museum of Art, Columbus, Ohio.

Study the pictures.

▶ Point to the shapes in this picture that are not geometric shapes.

🔍 **Aesthetic Perception**

Seeing Like an Artist Name a free-form shape you see. Trace the shape with your finger.

Using Free-Form Shapes

Artists use **free-form shapes** to show people, animals, and other things.

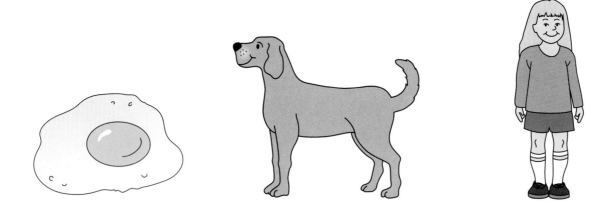

Practice

1. Look at the objects your teacher shows you.

2. Trace the shape of each object in the air.

▲ **Steven Roth.** Age 6.

Think about how the student used free-form shapes in this artwork.

Creative Expression

Where do you see free-form shapes in nature? Print some free-form shapes using leaves.

1. Roll ink onto leaves.

2. Press the leaves on your paper.

Art Criticism

Decide Which leaf shape do you think is most interesting? Why?

Lesson 4 More About Shapes

▲ **Allan Rohan Crite.** (American). *School's Out.* 1936.

Oil on canvas. $30\frac{1}{4} \times 36\frac{1}{8}$ inches (76.84 × 91.75 cm.). Smithsonian American Art Museum, Washington, D.C.

Look how you can find **geometric shapes** and **free-form shapes** outside.

 Art History and Culture

Sometimes artists create art to tell us about people and places they have seen.

▲ **Ben Shahn.** (American).
World's Greatest Comics.
1946.

Tempera on panel. 35 × 48 inches
(88.9 × 121.92 cm.). Amon Carter
Museum, Fort Worth, Texas.

Study the pictures.

▶ Find different shapes in the paintings
and name them.

Aesthetic Perception

Seeing Like an Artist Name a free-form shape
you see. Trace the shape with your finger.

Using Geometric and Free-Form Shapes

You can find different shapes everywhere you look.

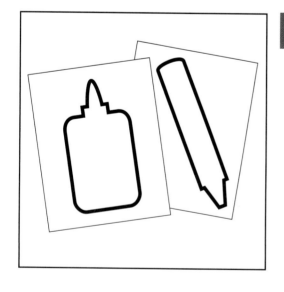

1. Look at the outlines of the objects.
2. Name the objects.

▲ **Barbara Kipreos.**
Age 5.

Think about the different geometric and free-form shapes the student used.

How many geometric shapes and free-form shapes can you find?

1. Draw a picture of your house. Use geometric shapes.

2. Draw the background with free-form shapes from nature.

Analyze What geometric and free-form shapes did you use?

Lesson 5 Body Shapes

Look at both works of art. The artists used shapes to show body parts. Body parts have many different shapes.

◀ **William H. Johnson.** (American). *Li'l Sis.* 1944.

Oil on paperboard. 26 × 21¼ inches (66.04 × 53.98 cm.). Smithsonian American Art Museum, Washington, D.C.

 Art History and Culture

The art of both artists helps us learn about the history of African Americans.

Study the pictures.

▶ Name the body parts you see in the pictures.

▲ **Jacob Lawrence.**
(American) *Harriet Tubman Series #4.*
1939–1940.
....
Casein tempera on gessoed hardboard, Hampton University Art Museum, Hampton, Virginia.

Aesthetic Perception

Seeing Like an Artist Is your hand a free-form shape or a geometric shape?

Using Free-Form Shapes

All body parts are **free-form shapes.**

Practice

1. Use your finger to trace around your head.

2. Trace around your foot. How is its shape different from your head?

Think about the kinds of free-form shapes this student used in her drawing.

◀ **Stephanie Gowdy.** Age 6.

How many free-form shapes does your body have?

1. Draw a big picture of yourself. Fill the entire sheet of paper.

2. Show how you look today. Draw the clothes you are wearing.

Describe What shapes did you use to create your self-portrait?

The Shape of People

Look at these works of art. The people are all different sizes. Some people are big. Some people are small.

◀ **Miriam Schapiro.** (Canadian American). *Father and Daughter.* 1997.
....
Acrylic and fabric on canvas. 72 × 60 inches (182.88 × 152.4 cm.). Private collection.

 Art History and Culture

Artists have different ways of showing people in their works of art. What are the people doing in these works of art?

Study the pictures.

▶ Point to the smallest person in each picture.

▶ Point to the biggest person in each picture.

◀ **Romare Bearden.**
(American). *Family.* 1988.
. . . .
Collage on wood. 28 × 20 inches
(71.12 × 50.8 cm.). Smithsonian
American Art Museum,
Washington, D.C.

 **Aesthetic Perception**

Seeing Like an Artist Who is the tallest person in the room?

Using Shapes to Create People

The **shapes** used to draw people are different sizes.

Practice

1. Sort the objects by size.
2. Draw shapes that are the same sizes as the objects.

◀ **Kaitlyn Erikanti.**
Age 6.

Think about who each person in the picture might be.

How many different people sizes do you have in your family?

1. Think about the size of people in your family.

2. Cut out different size shapes to show the people in your family.

3. Arrange the shapes on your paper.

Decide Do you think your family members will recognize themselves in your portrait? Why?

Shape

▲ **Leo Twiggs.** (American). *Big Blues Man II.*
1993.
. . . .
Batik painting on cotton. 24 × 19 inches (60.96 × 48.26 cm.).
Private collection.

Art Criticism | Critical Thinking

Describe

▶ What are the people doing?

Analyze

▶ What geometric shapes do you see in the painting? What free-form shapes do you see?

Interpret

▶ Who do you think are the other people with the Blues Man in the painting?

Decide

▶ Did this painting tell you a story?

Show What You Know

Answer these questions on a separate sheet of paper.

1 Which of these is a geometric shape?

A.

B.

2 Which of these is a free-form shape?

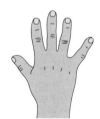
A.

B.

3 What kind of shapes are body parts?

A. geometric
B. free-form

CAREERS IN ART
Illustrator

Some artists create pictures to help us understand what we are reading.

Children's book illustrators draw pictures to help us understand what is happening in stories.

Advertising illustrators draw pictures of items that are for sale. They draw pictures for things like catalogs and food packages.

▲ **Book Illustrator**

Shape in Dance

Jerry Duke creates dances. His dancers make lots of circles. His dancers sometimes work with puppets.

What to Do Create circle shapes and forms.

1. Draw five circles of different sizes.

2. Make circles with your body.

3. Make circles with a partner.

4. Make a circle with a group.

5. Do a circle dance.

▲ AMAN International Folk Ensemble: "Suite of Appalachian Music and Dance."

Analyze How did you create circular shapes with a partner?

Color

◀ **Henri Matisse.**
(French). *Woman in a Purple Coat.* 1937.
. . . .
Oil on canvas.
$31\frac{7}{8} \times 25\frac{11}{16}$ inches
(80.9 × 65.2 cm.).
Museum of Fine Arts,
Houston, Houston,
Texas.

Colors are everywhere.

Look around you to find colors.

Artists use many different **colors** in their art. What colors in the painting can you name?

In This Unit you will:

▶ learn about colors.

▶ practice using them in your artwork .

Henri Matisse

(1869–1954)

▶ was a great French artist.

▶ loved to paint with bright colors.

A Garden of Colors

▲ **Peggy Flora Zalucha.** (American). *Sprinkler Garden.* 1994.
Transparent watercolor on paper. 36 × 52 inches (91.44 × 132.08 cm.). Courtesy of Peggy Flora Zalucha.

Look at the flower gardens. They are full of **colors.**

 Art History and Culture

The flowers in this painting look real. Artists sometimes paint in a realistic style.

Study the pictures.

▶ Does the second picture have any colors that you did not see in the first picture?

◀ **Edouard Vuillard.** (French). *Garden at Vaucresson.* 1937.

Tempera on canvas.
$59\frac{1}{2} \times 43\frac{5}{8}$ inches
(151.13 × 110.80 cm.).
The Metropolitan Museum of Art, New York, New York.

Aesthetic Perception

Seeing Like an Artist Look around you. What colors do you see?

Using Color

Colors have names.

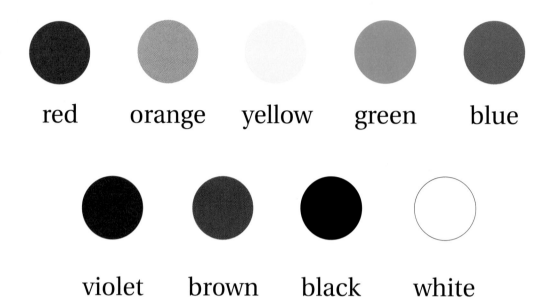

red   orange   yellow   green   blue

violet   brown   black   white

Practice

1. Look at the paper your teacher shows the class.

2. Show a crayon that matches the paper color.

▲ **Lauren Knutti.**
Age 5.

Think about the colors you see in this student's work.

Creative Expression

What colors would you put in your garden?

1. Think about the types of flowers you like best.

2. Draw your own flower garden.

Art Criticism

Decide Would your garden look real if you used only one color? Why?

Lesson 2 Recognizing Objects by Color

◀ **Audrey Flack.**
(American). *Energy
Apples.* 1980.
· · · · · · · · · · · · · · · · · · ·
Acrylic and oil on canvas.
$47\frac{3}{4} \times 48\frac{1}{4}$ inches (121.29
× 122.56 cm.). Private
Collection.

Look at both pictures. What kinds
of food do you see in these works
of art?

 Art History and Culture

Sometimes artists get ideas for their art from
objects they see every day. What everyday
objects are in these works of art?

▲ **Jacob Lawrence.** (American).
Still Life with Grapes and Roses.
1954.

Egg tempera on hardboard. $17\frac{3}{4} \times 23\frac{7}{8}$ inches
(45.09 × 58.42 cm.). Private collection.

Study the pictures.

▶ Would it be harder to name each
food if they were not colored?

 **Aesthetic Perception**

Seeing Like an Artist Look around. What
objects do you see that are the color red?

Using Color To Recognize Objects

Colors help us identify things.

Practice

1. Think about the color your teacher says.
2. Name food that is that color.

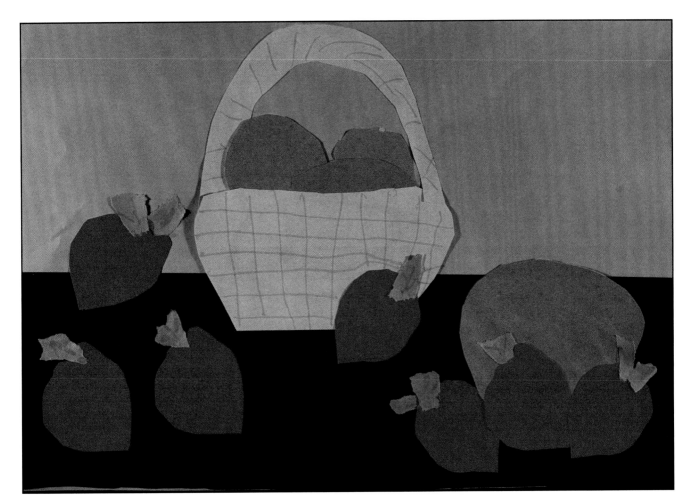

Think about the kinds of fruit you see in the student's artwork.

 **Creative Expression**

What kinds of fruit do you see?

1. Choose paper that matches the fruit colors.

2. Cut shapes and make a collage.

 **Art Criticism**

Describe What colors did you use for your collage?

Looking at Colors

Look at these works of art. Sometimes artists use many colors.

▲ **Wayne Thiebaud.**
(American). *Three Machines.* 1963.

Oil on canvas. 30 × 36$\frac{1}{2}$ inches (76.2 × 92.71 cm.). Fine Arts Museum of San Francisco, San Francisco, California.

 Art History and Culture

Chagall has made murals, stained-glass windows, and mosaics that help decorate buildings in different communities.

◀ **Marc Chagall.**
(Russian). *I and the Village.* 1911.
Oil on canvas. $75\frac{5}{8} \times 59\frac{5}{8}$ inches (192.1 × 151.4 cm.). Museum of Modern Art, New York, New York.

Study the pictures.

▶ How do you think the artists decided which colors to use?

🔍 Aesthetic Perception

Seeing Like an Artist What colors would you use to paint a picture of your favorite toy?

Using Colors

Artists use colors to make their artwork look interesting.

1. Find objects in the room that are the same color as your piece of paper.

2. Tell the class what you found.

▲ **Susan Morris.**
Age 5.

Think about what shape the student created in her collage.

 Creative Expression

Where can you find colors?

1. Create a collage using the color your teacher gives you.

2. Find that color in magazine pictures. Cut out pieces of that color to make your collage.

 Art Criticism

Describe Name the color that you collected. What shape did you create?

Primary Colors

◀ **Henri Matisse.** (French).
Music. 1939.

Oil on canvas. $45\frac{1}{4} \times 45\frac{3}{8}$ inches
(114.93 × 115.25 cm.). Albright-Knox
Art Gallery, Buffalo, New York.

Look at these works of art. They have
some of the same colors.

 Art History and Culture

Art like the *Octopus Bag* helps us learn what it
is like to live in different places and times.

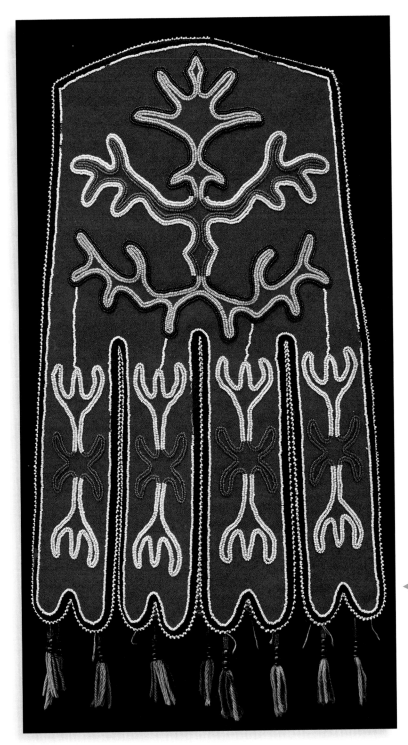

Study the pictures.

▶ Where do you see the colors red, yellow, and blue?

◀ **Artist Unknown.**
Tlingit. (Canadian.)
Octopus Bag.
c. 1890.
. . . .
Wool cloth, wool tape, glass
beads, yarn, cotton cloth
lining. $21\frac{1}{2}$ × 12 inches
(54.61 × 30.48 cm.).
Seattle Museum of Art,
Seattle, Washington.

Aesthetic Perception

Seeing Like an Artist Look around your
classroom. Do you see any objects that are red,
yellow, or blue?

Using Primary Colors

The **primary colors** are red, yellow, and blue. They are very special because no other colors can be mixed to make them. They are the first colors.

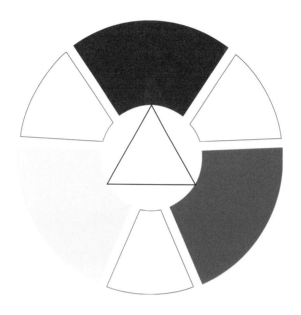

Practice

1. Look at the fabric your teacher gave you.

2. Decide which primary color you see the most on your fabric. Go to the corner of the room that shows that color.

Think about the colors you see in the student's drawing.

◀ **Jed Woodward.** Age 6.

 Creative Expression

What object will you draw?

1. Find an object you like.

2. Use red, yellow, and blue markers only. Draw and color a picture of your object.

 **Art Criticism**

Analyze What colors did you use? What are these colors called?

Lesson 5 Colors Show Feelings

Look at these paintings. Notice how the colors are different.

▲ **Janet Fish.** (American).
Feeding Caitlin. 1988.

Oil on canvas. $54\frac{1}{4} \times 70$ inches
(137.80 × 177.8 cm.). Butler
Institute of American Art,
Youngstown, Ohio.

 Art History and Culture

Artists use colors to help show feelings. During one period Picasso painted many blue paintings. Why do you think he chose blue?

Study the pictures.

▶ How does each painting make you feel?

◀ **Pablo Picasso.** (Spanish).
The Tragedy. 1903.
. . . .
Oil paint on wood. $41\frac{1}{2} \times 27$ inches (105.4 × 69 cm.). National Gallery of Art, Washington, D.C.

🔍 **Aesthetic Perception**

Seeing Like an Artist Name a creature you have seen in a cartoon. What color is it?

Using Color To Show Feelings

Artists use **bright colors** to make us feel happy.

Dull colors can make us feel sad or scared.

Practice

1. Look at the color your teacher shows you.

2. Show with your face how the color makes you feel.

▲ **Michael Olson.** Age 6.

▲ **Emily Wyatt.** Age 6.

Think about how these students' artwork makes you feel.

 Creative Expression

How do different colors make you feel?

1. Choose bright or dull colors for your portrait.

2. Draw your face and body. Then add details.

 Art Criticism

Interpret How do the colors in your picture make you feel? Give your picture a title.

Lesson 6 Light and Dark Colors

▲ **John Henry Twachtman.**
(American). *Waterfall Blue Brook.*
c. 1895–1900.
....
Oil on canvas. $25\frac{1}{8} \times 30\frac{1}{16}$ inches (63.81 × 77.72 cm.). Cincinnati Art Museum, Cincinnati, Ohio.

Look at the pictures of water. They have light and dark colors.

 Art History and Culture

Long ago Japanese prints were made by a team of four artists. Each person did one step to help make the print.

Study the works of art.

▶ Point to a dark blue part in the pictures. Now point to a light blue part.

◀ **Katsushika Hokusai.** (Japanese). *Kirifuri Waterfall on Mount Kurokami in Shimotsuke Province. c. 1833–1834*

Color woodblock print. $15\frac{5}{16}$ × $10\frac{3}{8}$ inches (38.9 × 26.3 cm.). Honolulu Academy of Arts, Honolulu, Hawaii.

🔍 Aesthetic Perception

Seeing Like an Artist Look in a book. Find a picture that has light green and dark green.

Using Light and Dark Colors

Mixing colors with black make them **darker.**

Mixing colors with white makes them **lighter.**

Practice

1. Mix one drop of black paint with blue.

2. Mix one drop of blue paint with white.

▲ **Yung Kipreos.**
Age 6.

Think about where you see light colors in the student's work. Where do you see dark colors?

What things in the sea have light and dark colors?

1. Create a sea picture with light and dark colors.

2. Add details like fish, waves, and plants.

Decide Do you like the light and dark colors in your painting? Which part do you like best?

▲ **Rodney Alan Greenblat.** (American).
Control Chair. 1986.
- -
Painted wood, leather, lights, electrical outlets, and casters.
39 × 26¾ × 27½ inches (99.06 × 67.95 × 69.85 cm.).
Birmingham Museum of Art, Birmingham, Alabama.

Describe

▶ What is this work of art?

Analyze

▶ What colors do you see on this chair?

Interpret

▶ What do you think it would feel like to sit in this chair?

Decide

▶ Do you think this chair is a work of art? Why or why not?

Show What You Know

Answer these questions on a sheet of paper.

1 Which of these is blue?

A.   B.

2 Which of these is a dull color?

A.   B.

3 Which of these would you add to make a color lighter?

A.   B.

LET'S VISIT A MUSEUM
The Yale University Gallery

This museum has art from all over the world. It is best known for its collection of paintings and works of art by American artists.

Color in Storytelling and Music

Paul Tracey is a storyteller. He tells stories about Africa. His stories teach people about right and wrong. In this story, each animal makes its own interesting sound.

What to Do Make the sounds and movements of some animals.

1. Make the African sounds for each animal.

2. Find a way to move like each animal as you say their sounds.

3. Make up your own sounds and movements for Eagle and Hyena.

4. Perform them for others.

▲ Paul Tracey.
"The Girl on the Rock"

 **Art Criticism**

Decide Were you successful in expressing different kinds of moods and feelings?

Space and Form

A form is a solid object that takes up space.

◀ **Allan Houser.** (American).
Earth Song. 1978.
. . . .
Alabama marble. 48 × 24 × 24 inches
(121.92 × 60.96 × 60.96 cm.). The
Herald Museum, Phoenix, Arizona.

You can see all around a form. There is space around the form.

▶ Point to a form in the picture.

▶ Point to space in the picture.

In This Unit you will:

▶ learn about space and form.

▶ practice using them in your artwork.

Allan Houser
(1914–1994)

▶ was a Native American artist.

▶ was an art teacher.

▶ painted before he became a sculptor.

1 Space in Art

▲ **Raoul Dufy.** (French). *Le Pantheon et Saint-Etienne-du-Mont.* c. 1903–1906.

Oil on canvas. $25\frac{1}{2} \times 31\frac{1}{4}$ inches (64.77 × 79.38 cm.). Albright-Knox Art Gallery, Buffalo, New York.

Look at the many shapes artists use in their art. **Space** is the empty area between shapes.

 Art History and Culture

Hopper liked to paint pictures of objects and places that are familiar to people, such as towns, trains, and stores.

Study the pictures.

▶ Point to empty areas around the shapes in the works of art.

Aesthetic Perception

Seeing Like an Artist Do you see space around the clouds when you look in the sky?

Using Space in Art

The empty places around and between shapes are called **space.**

1. Hold hands with your partner. Notice the space between you.

2. Stand back to back with your partner. What happened to the space?

▲ **Zoe Lequeux.** Age 5.

Think about where you see space in this student's art.

 Creative Expression

How could you show space on paper?

1. Draw a landscape with trees or houses.

2. Color the sky.

 Art Criticism

Interpret Is it daytime or nighttime in your picture? How can you tell?

Look at this form. It is a **sculpture.** It has a front, back, top, bottom, and sides.

◄ **Felipa Trujillo.** (American). *Man.* Early 1900s.

Museum of International Folk Art, a unit of the Museum of New Mexico, Santa Fe, New Mexico.

 Art History and Culture

This artist was taught how to make pottery by people in her family. What has someone in your family taught you?

Study both sculptures.

▶ Describe what you think each one would look like from all sides.

Aesthetic Perception

Seeing Like an Artist What are the different sides of a form you see in your classroom?

Using Forms

A **form** is a solid. You can look all around a form.

Practice

1. Draw your favorite thing in the classroom.

2. Look at your drawing next to the real object.

◄ **Aaron Ragans.**
Age 6.

Think about what you might see if you looked at this artwork from the side.

 Creative Expression

What do you look like from different sides?

1. Make a clay form of yourself.
2. Use a pencil to add a face and clothing.

 Art Criticism

Analyze Does your sculpture have a front, back, top, bottom, and sides?

Space and Form

▲ **Henry Moore.**
(British). *Reclining Figure.* 1939.

Elm. 37 inches high (93.98 cm.). Detroit Institute of The Arts, Detroit, Michigan.

Look at how space is used in all the forms in these works of art. Space is above, below, and through the forms.

 Art History and Culture

Different artists like to make sculptures in different ways. Some sculptures look like real people.

▲ **Duane Hanson.** (American).
Old Couple on a Bench. 1994–1995.

Bronze, polychromed, mixed media with
accessories. Palm Springs Desert Museum,
Palm Springs, California.

Study the pictures.

▶ Where do you see forms in the pictures?

▶ Where do you see space?

Aesthetic Perception

Seeing Like an Artist Point to the space around a form in your classroom.

Using Space and Form

The empty areas around and through a form are **space.**

1. Look at a stuffed animal.

2. Point to the space around the animal.

◄ **Sarah Stewart.**
Age 6.

Think about where you see space around the student's puppet.

Where is the space around your puppet?

1. Practice holding and moving your paper-towel tube.

2. Use the tube to make a puppet.

Interpret Is your puppet more like the sculpture of the man and woman, or is it more like the wood sculpture? Why?

Lesson 4 · A Building Is a Form

▲ **Frank Lloyd Wright.** (American). *Stockman House.* 1908.
. . . .
Mason City, Iowa.

Look at these pictures of buildings. Buildings are forms with many different parts.

 Art History and Culture

Artists who design buildings are called **architects.** What kinds of buildings have you visited?

Study the pictures.

▶ Name some of the different parts of these buildings.

Aesthetic Perception

Seeing Like an Artist What parts of your school building do you see when you are outside?

Using Building Forms

A building is a **form.** You can walk around and inside a building and see all the parts.

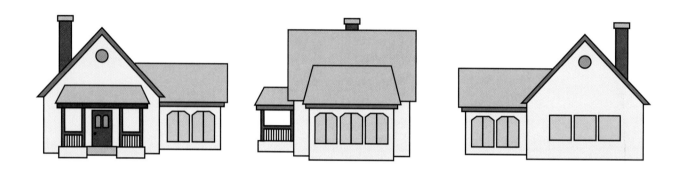

1. Think about the buildings you saw on your way to school.
2. Draw one of the buildings you saw.

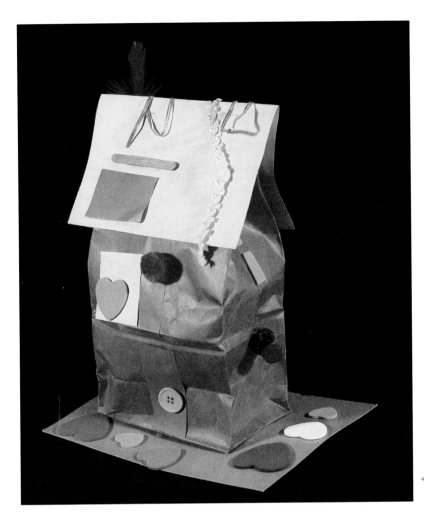

Think about the different parts you see in this house.

◄ **Anwesha Nandi.**
Age 5.

Creative Expression

What kinds of houses have you seen? Design your own house.

1. Fill the paper bag with newspaper. Staple a folded piece of paper to the top so it looks like a roof.

2. Decorate your house with doors and windows.

Decide What parts might you add to make your house more interesting?

An Animal Is a Form

Look at these animals. Sometimes artists make forms of animals. We can look at every side of animal forms.

◀ **Artist Unknown.** (China.) *Bactrian Camel with Packsaddle.* C. A.D. 700–750.
....
Earthenware with three-colored glaze. 36⅛ inches high (91.75 cm.). Nelson Atkins Museum, Kansas City, Missouri.

 Art History and Culture

These animals are very old works of art. Why do you think they have been kept for so many years?

Study the pictures.

▶ What kinds of animal forms do you
see in the pictures?

Aesthetic Perception

Seeing Like an Artist What other animals with
four legs could be made as a sculpture?

Using Animal Forms

An animal **sculpture** is a **form.** You can walk around this animal form and see all four legs.

Practice

1. Draw an animal with four legs.
2. Count the legs.

◀ **Davis Hays.**
Age 6.

Think about the kind of animal form this student made.

 **Creative Expression**

What do your favorite animals look like? Design an animal form.

1. Make an animal with four legs out of clay.

2. Use a pencil to add eyes and other details.

 **Art Criticism**

Interpret What is your animal doing? What sound would it make if it could speak?

Lesson 6 Forms Can Be Used

◄ **Artist Unknown.** (China.) *Painted Storage Jar.* c. 2500–1700 B.C.

Clay, iron oxide, and magnesium pigments. 15 inches high × 16 inches in diameter (38.1 × 40.64 cm.). Kimbell Art Museum, Fort Worth, Texas.

Look at these works of art.
Artwork can be pretty and useful.

 Art History and Culture

Sometimes artists make forms that can be used to do a job. What forms do you have at home that can be used to do a job?

▲ **Artist Unknown.** (Native American, Cherokee or Iroquois.) *Bowl.* c. 1800.
. . . .
Wood and brass. $13\frac{5}{8}$ inches high (34.60 cm.). Detroit Institute of the Arts, Detroit, Michigan.

Study the pictures.

▶ How would you use the forms in the pictures?

🔍 **Aesthetic Perception**

Seeing Like an Artist Where do you see forms that are pretty and useful?

Using Forms

Jars and bowls are **forms** that people look at and use.

Practice

1. Flatten the clay your teacher gives you.

2. Did you use both hands or just one?

◄ **Elizabeth Sterling Morris.** Age 5.

Think about how you could use this student's pot.

 **Creative Expression**

How could you design a piece of art to use at home? Create a pinch pot.

1. Pinch your clay ball to form a pot.

2. Use a pencil to make a design on your pot.

 **Art Criticism**

Interpret What will you keep inside your pinch pot?

Space and Form

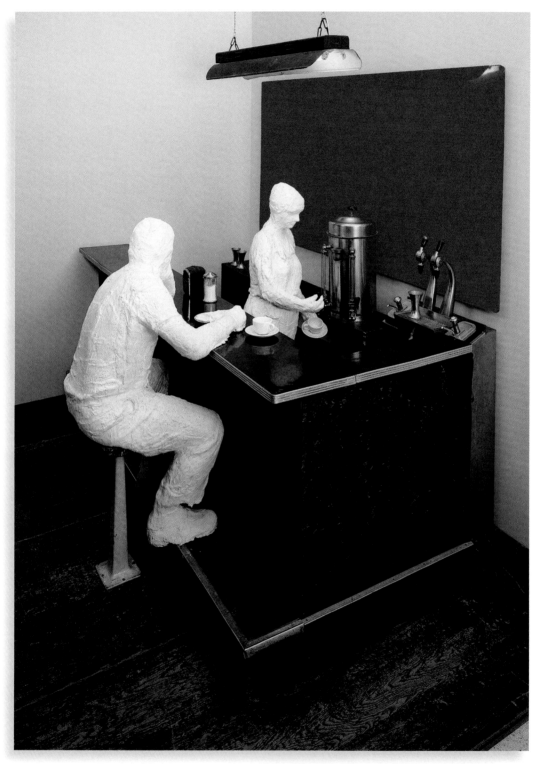

▲ **George Segal.** (American). *The Diner.*
1964–1966.

. . . .

Plaster, wood, chrome, laminated plastic, masonite, and
fluorescent lamp. $98\frac{3}{4} \times 144\frac{1}{4} \times 96$ inches ($250.83 \times 366.40 \times 243.84$ cm.). The Walker Art Center, Minneapolis, Minnesota.

Art Criticism Critical Thinking

Describe

▶ How many people do you see in the sculpture?

Analyze

▶ Where do you see space around the people?

Interpret

▶ What do you think the people are saying to each other?

Decide

▶ Does this look like a place you would like to go to get something to eat?

Space and Form, continued

Show What You Know

Answer these questions on a sheet of paper.

1 Which of these works of art is a form?

A.

B.

2 Which of these is **not** a form?

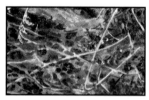
A.

B.

3 A form can be seen

A. from all sides.
B. from only the front.

Motion Pictures

Do you like to watch movies? Artists help create movies.

Animators draw still pictures and make them look like they are moving, like you see in a cartoon.

Make-up artists put make-up on actors to change how they look.

▲ **Animator**

Space and Form in Music and Dance

▲ Ranganiketan Manipuri Cultural Arts Troupe. *Dhon Dholak Cholam.*

These drummers dance as they play music. They leap around a circle.

What to Do Create a dance that includes clapping and stomping.

1. Make clapping patterns that have long (ta) and short (ti-ti) sounds.

2. Try walking on just the *ta* sounds. Try walking on just the *ti-ti* sounds.

3. Make up your own sound patterns with *ta* and *ti-ti*. Walk in the same rhythm that you are saying with your voice.

4. Watch and listen to your teacher. Repeat what your teacher did.

 **Art Criticism**

Describe What movements did you do to match the sounds you made?

Texture

▲ **Beau Dick.** (Kwakwaka'wakw Tribe, Canadian). *Urban Raven/Urban Indian Transformation Mask.* 2002.

Hand-carved and painted red cedar. 10 × 12 × 23 inches when closed (25.4 × 30.48 × 58.42 cm.). Douglas Reynolds Gallery, Vancouver, British Columbia.

Texture is the way something feels.

Artists use different materials to create texture. Some texture is real. You can feel it. Some texture can be seen but not felt.

▶ How do you think this mask feels to the touch?

In This Unit you will:

▶ learn about texture.

▶ see how artists use texture on their works of art.

▶ use texture on your artwork.

Beau Dick

(1955–   )

Beau Dick

▶ is a member of the Tsawataineuk First Nation.

▶ carves masks, poles, rattles, and talking sticks.

▶ learned to carve from his father and grandfather.

Lesson 1 Texture You Can Touch

Look at the works of art. They are made of wood.

◄ **Betty Parsons.** (American).
Winged Frog. 1978.

Mixed-media wood construction. 27 × 20 inches
(68.58 × 50.8 cm.). The National Museum of
Women in the Arts, Washington, D.C.

 Art History and Culture

Betty Parsons was an artist and an art dealer.
She had a gallery where she showed other
artists' works of art.

Study both works of art.

▶ Which parts look rough?

▶ Which parts look smooth?

◀ **John Hoover.** (Native American, Aleut). *Eagle and Salmon.* 1987.
Cedar. 48 × 24 inches (121.92 × 60.96 cm.).
Private Collection.

Aesthetic Perception

Seeing Like an Artist Describe how textures in your classroom feel.

Using Real Texture

Something you can feel with your fingers is called **real texture.**

Practice

1. Feel each object your teacher shows you.

2. Use one word to tell how each object feels.

▲ **Grayson Gunn.** Age 5.

Think about the kinds of texture you see in the student's artwork. How would these textures feel?

Creative Expression

How many different textures can you put in a **collage** ?

1. Think about the shapes you see in a landscape.

2. Cut out the shapes.

3. Use these shapes to make a landscape with textures.

Art Criticism

Analyze How many different real textures are there in your collage? Describe how the different textures in your collage feel to the touch.

Texture You Can See

Look at the paintings. Can you see texture?

◀ **Gabriele Münter.**
(German). *Child with Ball.*
c. 1916.
. . . .
Oil on canvas. 20 $\frac{1}{2}$ × 17 inches
(52.07 × 43.18 cm.). The National
Museum of Women in the Arts,
Washington, D.C.

 Art History and Culture

Do you think the people in the paintings are from now or long ago? Why?

Study both pictures.

▶ How do you think the child's hat would feel?

▶ How do you think the woman's coat would feel?

◀ **Jean Etienne Liotard.** (Swiss). *Portrait of Marthe Marie Tronchin.* c. 1758–1761.

Pastel and stumping on vellum. $24\frac{9}{16} \times 18\frac{5}{8}$ inches (62.38 × 47.30 cm.). The Art Institute of Chicago, Chicago, Illinois.

Aesthetic Perception

Seeing Like an Artist How could you draw the texture of something you see?

Using Visual Texture

Texture you can see but cannot touch is **visual texture.**

Practice

1. Feel the bottom of your shoe.
2. What kinds of lines would you use to draw the bottom of your shoe?

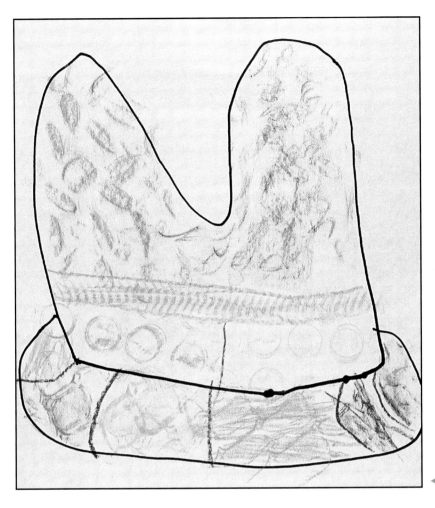

Think about the kinds of lines the student used to show texture.

◄ **Catherine Burton.** Age 5.

How can you show how different things feel?

1. Design a hat that has different textures.

2. Make crayon rubbings to create different textures.

Interpret Who might wear the hat you made?

Designing with Texture

◀ **Artist Unknown.** (Western Europe). *Hand Puppets.* Late nineteenth century.
....
Painted wood. 16 inches high on average (40.64 cm.). Museum of International Folk Art, Santa Fe, New Mexico.

Look at the art on both pages. The artists used texture on these toys.

 Art History and Culture

Artists have made puppets and toys for a long time. Puppets are often used for telling stories.

Study the puppets and toys.

▶ Name the kinds of textures you see on the heads and bodies of the puppets and toys.

Aesthetic Perception

Seeing Like an Artist Tell about the textures of a puppet or toy you have seen.

Using Texture

Cloth and yarn have different **textures.**

1. Feel your sleeve.
2. How does it feel?

Think about the different textures you see in the artwork.

◀ **Rose Valentine.** Age 5.

Where would you place different textures on a puppet?

1. Think about a puppet you would like to make.

2. Choose textured materials for your puppet.

3. Glue the materials on your paper bag.

Interpret Is your puppet feeling happy? Scared? Sad? Silly? Give your puppet a name.

Fiber Textures

◀ **Artist Unknown.**
(United States).
Appalachian Basket.
1988.
. . . .
Split oak. 12 × 12 inches
(30.48 × 30.48 cm.). Hudak
Private Collection.

Look at the baskets in the
pictures. Baskets have texture.

 Art History and Culture

People from all over the world weave baskets.
Why do you think people make baskets?

Study the basket pictures.

▶ How would each basket feel to touch?

Aesthetic Perception

Seeing Like an Artist Straw is a fiber. What other fibers could be used to weave a basket?

▲ **Artist Unknown.** (Native American, Pomoan). *Gift Basket.* c. 1870–1880.

Sedge, bulrush root, woodpecker tufts. $4\frac{1}{2} \times 9\frac{1}{2}$ inches (11.43 × 24.13 cm.). Lowe Art Museum, Miami, Florida.

Using Fiber Textures

Wood, straw, and grass are **fiber textures.**

Practice

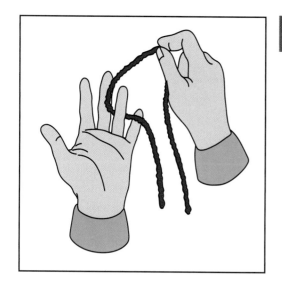

1. Watch as your teacher shows you how to weave.

2. Practice weaving through your fingers with yarn.

Think about the baskets the student made. What kind of fibers did she use to add texture to the baskets?

Creative Expression

What fibers would you use to make a basket?

1. Choose a fiber.
2. Weave the fiber through the slits in the cup.

Art Criticism

Decide What will you keep in your basket?

Lesson 5 Real Texture on Forms

▲ **Artist Unknown.** Ashanti people. (Ghana). *Fish, Gold Weight.* Nineteenth–twentieth century.
· ·
Brass. $3\frac{1}{2}$ inches high (8.89 cm.). The Metropolitan Museum of Art, New York, New York.

Look at the forms on these pages. The artists added texture to their forms.

 Art History and Culture

Long ago the Ashanti people used objects like this fish to weigh their gold. They also used objects like this to help them tell stories.

Study the forms on these pages.

▶ What do you think the fish would feel like if you touched it?

▶ Would the container feel the same as the fish?

◀ **Artist Unknown.** (China). *Ritual Wine Container.*
Thirteenth century B.C.

Bronze. $11\frac{7}{8} \times 4\frac{3}{4} \times 4\frac{7}{8}$ inches (30.15 × 12.07 × 12.37 cm.).
Arthur M. Sackler Gallery, Smithsonian Institution, Washington, D.C.

Aesthetic Perception

Seeing Like an Artist What kinds of lines would you use to make a clay tiger?

Using Real Texture on Forms

Tools or objects can be used to add **texture** to artwork. The texture that you can feel is called **real texture.**

Practice

1. Find something around you that has raised or carved lines.

2. Tell how the lines make texture on the object.

◄ **Madalyn Kuhn.**
Age 4.
◄ **Matthew Ellett.**
Age 4.
◄ **Bobby Tucker.**
Age 5.

Think about the textures on the students' forms. How do you think the students created the textures?

 **Creative Expression**

What objects would you use to show real texture?

1. Roll a ball of clay, and then flatten it.

2. Shape the clay into a circle, square, or rectangle.

3. Press objects into the clay to create texture.

 **Art Criticism**

Describe What objects did you use to create textures in your design?

Lesson 6 Texture on Shapes

◀ **Harriet Powers.**
(American). *Bible Quilt, Detail: Dark Day of May 19, 1780.* c. 1897
....
Pieced and appliquéd cotton embroidered with plain and metallic yarns. 69 × 105 inches overall (175.26 × 266.7 cm.). Museum of Fine Arts, Boston, Massachusetts.

Look at the works of art on both pages. The artists added texture to the shapes on each cloth.

 Art History and Culture

Quilting has been a popular art form for a long time. The pictures in quilts often tell a story.

Study the shapes on the works of art.

▶ Point to the shapes the artists created
with yarn on these cloths. This art is
called **stitchery.**

Aesthetic Perception

Seeing Like an Artist What shapes did the
artists stitch in the pictures?

Using Texture on Shapes

Artists sew yarn to add **real texture** to artwork.

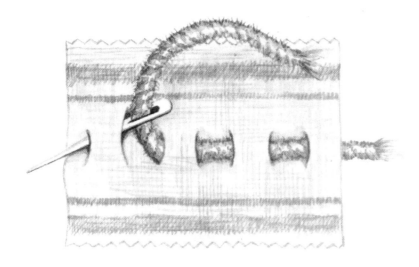

Practice

1. Watch as your teacher shows you how to sew.

2. Practice sewing some stitches.

◀ **Rachel Van Amburgh.**
Age 6.

Think about the shapes in the student's artwork. How did the student make texture on the shapes?

What kind of designs can you sew on cloth?

1. Think of some shapes you could sew.

2. Draw the shapes on your piece of burlap.

3. Sew along the outlines of your shapes.

Decide What else might you add to your stitchery?

Texture

▲ **Peggy Flora Zalucha.** (American). *My Dad's Violin.* 1998.

Watercolor on paper. 20 × 40 inches. (50.8 × 101.6 cm.). Private Collection.

Art Criticism Critical Thinking

Describe

▶ What musical instruments do you see?

Analyze

▶ What textures do you see?

Interpret

▶ Why are these things together in one painting?

Decide

▶ Does this work look real?

Show What You Know

Answer these questions on a separate sheet of paper.

1 Which of these has a bumpy texture?

A.

B.

2 Which of these was made with a fiber?

A.

B.

3 Which of these would you use to add texture on cloth?

A.

B.

LET'S VISIT A MUSEUM
The Nelson-Atkins Museum

This museum is in Kansas City, Missouri. It houses art from all over the world.

Texture in Music and Dance

▲ Korean Classical Music and Dance Company. *Korean Classical Music and Dance* and *Toraji Taryong.*

Korean folk music and dance have been around for more than 2,000 years. The songs and dances have been passed on from person to person.

What to Do Create a fan dance.

1. Make a fan and decorate it.

2. Hold the fan in one hand. Find five different ways to move it.

3. Hold the fan in both hands. Find three different ways to move with your fan.

4. Share your fan movements with a partner. Try each other's ideas.

Interpret How did you feel as you moved with your fan?

Principles of Art

Artists organize art using principles of art.

▶ What has the artist repeated on the pottery?

In This Unit you will:

▶ learn about pattern, rhythm, balance, and unity.

▶ see how artists use pattern, rhythm, balance, and unity in their works of art.

▶ use pattern, rhythm, balance, and unity in your artwork.

Maria Martínez

▶ was from New Mexico.

▶ was a Pueblo potter.

▶ had her husband decorate her pottery.

Lesson 1 Pattern

Look at these buildings. Artists help create buildings.

◄ **Artist Unknown.** (United States).
Victorian House. Late 19th century.
Atlanta, Georgia.

 Art History and Culture

These buildings were designed by **architects.**
Architects are artists who draw designs for
homes and other buildings.

Study both buildings.

▶ What kinds of lines are repeated?

▶ What kinds of shapes are repeated?

▶ What colors do you see?

◀ **Louis H. Sullivan.**
(United States).
Wainwright Building.
1890–1891.
St. Louis, Missouri.

Aesthetic Perception

Design Awareness Find lines, shapes, and colors that repeat on your clothes.

Using Pattern

Repeating lines, shapes, or colors creates **patterns.**

Practice

1. Think about different shapes.
2. Draw a pattern using two different shapes.

▲ **Tymber Moss.** Age 5.

Think about the patterns you see in the student's drawing.

Are there any patterns on your home?

1. Draw a picture of your home.

2. Add patterns to your home.

Analyze Which shapes, lines, or colors did you repeat?

Rhythm and Movement

▲ **Jack Savitsky.** (American). *Train in Coal Town.* 1968.

Oil on fiberboard. 31¼ × 47¾ inches (79.38 × 121.29 cm.). Smithsonian American Art Museum, Washington, D.C.

Look at the trains. They look like they are moving.

 Art History and Culture

Art can help us learn about life a long time ago. These pictures show us a time when many people used to travel by train.

▲ **Currier and Ives.** (American). *American Express Train.* 1864.

16 × 24⅞ inches (40.64 × 63.20 cm.). Museum of the City of New York. New York, New York.

Study both train pictures.

► What shapes did the artists repeat?

Aesthetic Perception

Seeing Like an Artist What shapes would you repeat to show a car or a boat moving?

Using Rhythm and Movement

Repeated shapes will create a sense of **rhythm** and **movement.**

1. Think about a train's wheels.
2. Move your arms like a train's wheels moving on a track.

▲ **Kyle Farren.** Age 5.

Think about the rhythm you see in the student's drawing. How did the student make the trains look like they are moving?

 **Creative Expression**

How can you show movement in your drawing?

1. Draw train tracks on your paper.
2. Draw a train on your tracks.

 **Art Criticism**

Decide Does your train create a sense of rhythm and movement? Is there anything else you might add to show more movement?

Lesson 3 Balance

Look at the butterfly. One half looks the same as the other half.

▲ **Artist Unknown.**
(China). *Butterfly.*
c. 1950.
Cut paper. $8\frac{1}{2} \times 15\frac{1}{8}$ inches
(21.59 × 38.41 cm.). Museum of
International Folk Art, Santa Fe,
New Mexico.

 Art History and Culture

Artists have been making cut paper designs in many countries for many years. The designs are often used as decorations for celebrations.

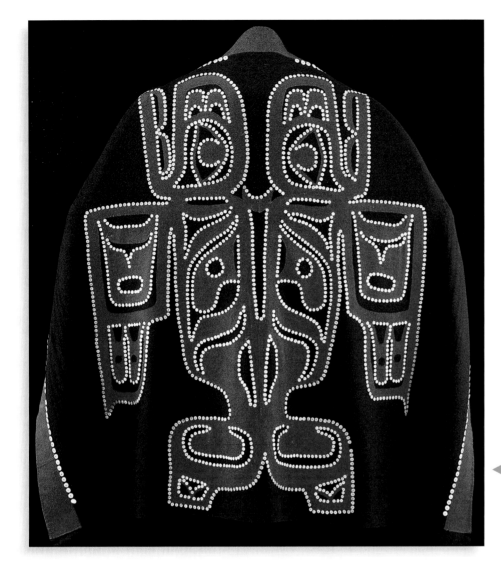

◄ **John Yeiltatzie.** (Haida).
Button Robe–Orca Whale Design. c. 1890.
∙∙∙∙∙∙∙∙∙∙∙∙∙∙∙∙∙∙∙∙∙∙∙∙∙∙∙∙∙∙∙∙
54 × 70 inches (137.16 × 177.8 cm.).
Seattle Art Museum, Seattle, Washington.

Study both pictures.

▶ Describe the parts of the butterfly that are the same on each half.

▶ Describe the parts of the whale design that are the same on each half.

Aesthetic Perception

Seeing Like an Artist What other animals can you name that have even balance?

Using Balance

An animal has **even balance.** The left half and the right half of an animal are the same.

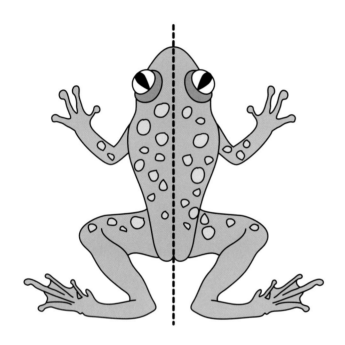

Practice

1. Pretend you are a bird.
2. Move your arms like a bird's wings flapping.
3. What body parts give the bird balance?

◄ **Rachel Perkins.** Age 5.

Think about the balance you see in the student's design.

How can you make a balanced design with paper and scissors?

1. Fold your paper in half the long way.

2. Cut shapes into the unfolded edge.

Analyze Does your design have balance? Why or why not?

Balance in Sculpture

Look at these sculptures. Do they have balance?

◀ **Artist Unknown.** (China).
Ritual Bell. 12th century B.C.
....
Bronze. $12\frac{3}{16} \times 9\frac{3}{4} \times 6$ inches (30.96 × 24.77 × 15.24 cm.). Arthur M. Sackler Gallery, Smithsonian Institution, Washington, D.C.

 Art History and Culture

House posts like the one on the next page are carved by the owner of the house. The pictures on the post tell a story about the family who lives in the house.

Study both pictures.

▶ Describe the parts of the bell that are the same on each half.

▶ Describe the parts of the house post that are the same on each half.

◀ **Artist Unknown.** (North America). *House Post.* 19th century.
....
$111\frac{1}{2} \times 38\frac{3}{16}$ inches (283.21 × 97 cm.). Seattle Art Museum, Seattle, Washington.

Aesthetic Perception

Design Awareness Look around you. What forms do you see that have balance?

Using Balance

Sculptures can have **balance.**
Sometimes parts on the left half and the
right half are the same.

Practice

1. Form a group of five.
2. Arrange your bodies to create a balanced live sculpture.

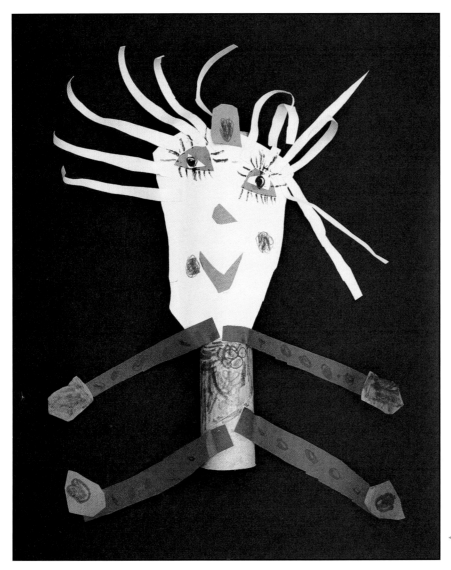

Think about how the student used balance in her house post.

◀ **Lorayna Hinton.**
Age 5.

What kind of house post would you make for your house?

1. Cut shapes for the face, arms, and legs of the creature.

2. Glue them to the tube so they are balanced.

Interpret What story does your house post tell?

Unity

▲ **Diego Rivera.** (Mexican).
Zandunga Tehuantepec Dance.
c. 1935.
....
Charcoal and watercolor. 19 × 24 inches
(48.1 × 60.6 cm.). Los Angeles County
Museum of Art, Los Angeles, California.

Look at these paintings. What is
happening in each picture?

 Art History and Culture

These artists are from similar cultures, but their
style of painting is very different.

▲ **Carmen Lomas Garza.**
(American). *Dance at El Jardin.* 1995.

Alkyds and oils on canvas.
24 × 32 inches (60.96 × 81.28 cm.). Private Collection.

Study both pictures.

▶ Name the objects you see in the first picture. Do they belong together?

▶ Name the objects you see in the second picture. Do they belong together?

Aesthetic Perception

Seeing Like an Artist What objects could you draw in a picture about school?

Using Unity

When a work of art has **unity,** it looks like everything belongs together.

1. Look at the objects your teacher shows you.
2. Which objects belong together?

◄ **Paul Hulett.**
Age 5.

Think about how the student showed unity in his drawing.

 Creative Expression

How can you show unity in your drawing?

1. Use the shape tool and line tool to show couples dancing.

2. Draw clothes and other details on your picture.

 Art Criticism

Analyze What did you do to help your drawing have unity?

Lesson 6 Unity in Sculpture

▲ **Sandy Skoglund.** (American).
The Green House. 1990.
....
Cibachrome color print. $46\frac{1}{4} \times 63$ inches
(117.48 × 160.02 cm.).

Look at these works of art.
Do they have unity?

 Art History and Culture

Sandy Skoglund used clay to create all the dogs
in this work of art.

▲ **Artist Unknown.**
(China). *Four Ladies of the Court Playing Polo.* 8th century.
. . . .
Painted terra cotta. 10 inches high (25.4 cm.). Nelson-Atkins Museum of Art, Kansas City, Missouri.

Study both pictures.

▶ Why do you think the artist made most of the dogs blue?

▶ How are the sculptures alike in the second picture?

Aesthetic Perception

Design Awareness What objects are repeated in your classroom?

Using Unity in Sculpture

Colors and forms that are alike help create **unity** in sculpture.

Practice

1. Look at pictures in magazines.
2. Cut out pictures that would create unity in a work of art.

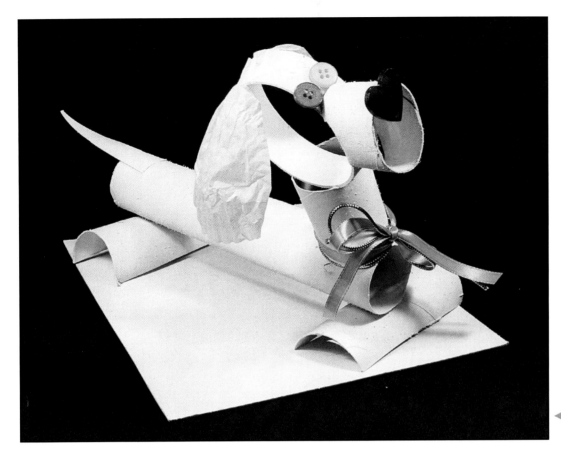

◄ **Alec Coleman.**
Age 5.

Think about what makes unity in this work of art.

 Creative Expression

How can you show unity with sculpture?

1. Use cardboard tubes to make an animal sculpture.

2. Arrange your sculpture with your classmates' sculptures to make one work of art.

 Art Criticism

Analyze Does the arrangement of sculptures have unity? Why or why not?

Principles of Art

▲ **Joseph Stella.** (Italian-American). *The Brooklyn Bridge: Variations on an Old Theme.* 1939.

Oil on canvas. 70 × 42 inches (177.8 × 106.68 cm.). Whitney Museum of American Art, New York, New York.

Art Criticism   Critical Thinking

Describe

▶ What do you see in the painting?

Analyze

▶ Where do you see a pattern of repeated shapes?

Interpret

▶ What do you think this painting is about?

Decide

▶ Does this painting make you think?

Show What You Know

Answer these questions on a separate sheet of paper.

1 Which of these shows a pattern?

A.   B.

2 Which of these has even balance?

 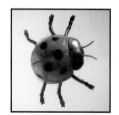

A.   B.

3 Which group of objects has unity?

A.   B.

CAREERS IN ART
Artists

Some artists earn a living by selling their art. Making art is their job.

Painters use paint to create pictures on flat surfaces, such as paper, canvas, or silk.

Sculptors are artists who make sculptures. A sculpture is a form that we can look at from every side.

▲ **Painter**

Rhythm, Balance, and Unity in Dance

Chuna McIntyre is a Yup'ik Eskimo. When he was young, his grandmother told him stories. In these stories the sun, moon, and animals sang and danced.

What to Do Mirror simple movements with a partner.

1. Find a partner. Decide who will be the leader and who will be the mirror.

2. The leader should start by slowly moving his or her arms. The mirror should imitate the leader.

3. Add more slow movements with other body parts. Then add strong movements.

4. Take turns being the leader and the mirror.

▲ Chuna McIntyre. *Brother Sun, Sister Moon.*

Analyze What made it possible for you and your partner to move together?

Technique Tips
Drawing
Pencil

Thin lines

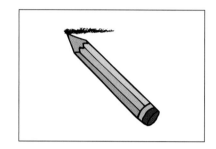

Thick lines

Crayon

Thin lines

Thick lines

Large spaces

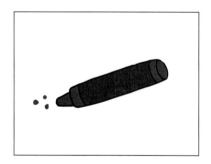

Small dots

Large dots

Technique Tips

Crayon Rubbing

Rub away from your holding hand.

Marker

Use the tip.

Use the side of the tip.

Put on the cap.

Technique Tips

Oil Pastel

Lines

Color in
large spaces.

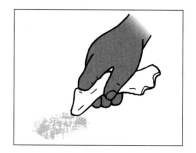

Blend colors.

Colored Chalk

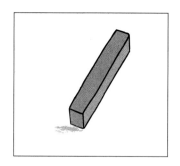

Lines

Color in
large spaces.

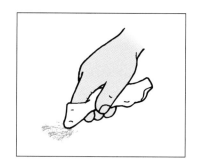

Blend colors.

Painting

Taking Care of Your Paintbrush

Rinse and blot to
change colors.

Technique Tips

Taking Care of Your Paintbrush

Clean your brush when you are done.

1. Rinse.

2. Wash with soap.

3. Rinse again.

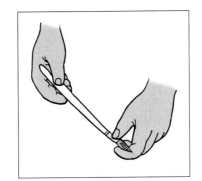

4. Shape.

5. Store.

Technique Tips

Tempera

Wipe the brush.

Mix the paint on a palette.

Use a wide brush for large spaces.

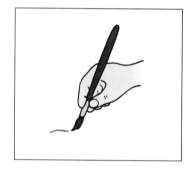

Use a thin, pointed brush for details.

Technique Tips

Watercolor

Put water on each color.

Dip the brush in the paint.

Mix on a palette.

Press firmly for thick lines.

Press lightly for thin lines.

Watercolor Resist

Crayons and oil pastels show through.

Technique Tips

Painting Rough Texture with Watercolor

1. Dip the brush in water.

2. Hold the brush over a container. Squeeze water out.

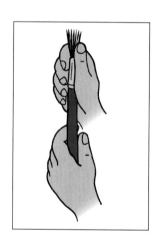

3. Divide the bristles into spikes.

4. Dip the brush in paint. Lightly touch the brush to paper.

5. Rinse. Shape the bristles into a point.

Technique Tips

Collage

Using Scissors

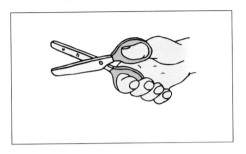

Hold scissors this way.

Hold the paper by its edge with your other hand.

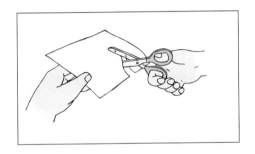

Always cut away from your body.

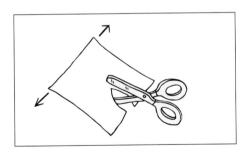

Have a friend stretch cloth as you cut.

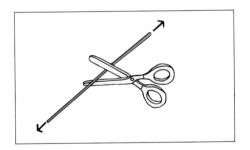

Do the same with yarn.

Technique Tips

Using Glue

Use only a few glue dots on one paper.

Smooth with the tip of the glue bottle.

Press the papers together.

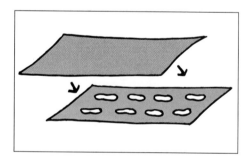

Close the bottle and clean the top.

Technique Tips

Arranging a Design

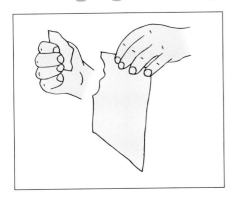

Tear shapes.

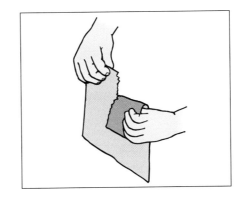

Tear strips.

Cut shapes.

Use found objects.

Make a design.

Glue the pieces
into place.

Technique Tips

Paper Sculpture

Making Strip Forms

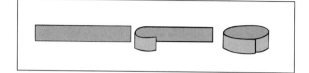

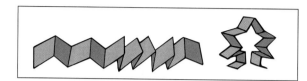

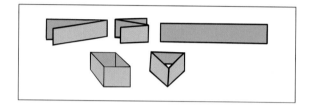

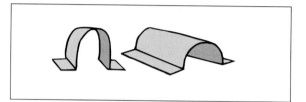

Use paper strips to make stairs, stars, tunnels, and other things.

Cones

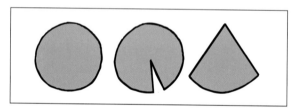

Building with Forms

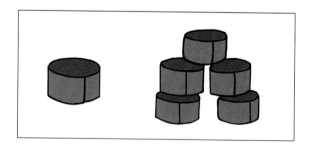

Technique Tips

Weaving

Making a Paper Loom

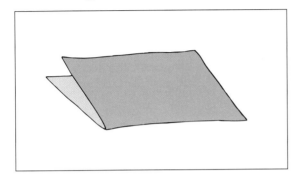

1. Fold paper in half.

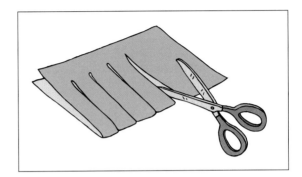

2. Cut wide strips from the folded edge. Don't cut to the other edge.

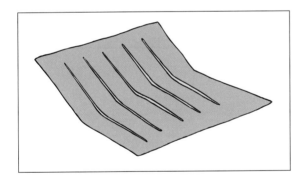

3. Open the paper.

Weaving on a Paper Loom

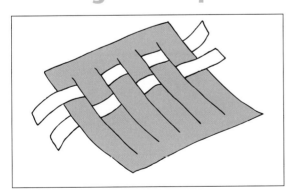

Over and under.

Technique Tips

Printmaking

Making a Stamp Print

1. Paint the stamp.

Or, press the stamp into a paint-filled sponge.

2. Press the stamp onto paper and lift.

Using a Brayer

1. Roll the brayer through the ink.

2. Roll the brayer over a leaf.

3. Press the leaf onto paper and lift.

Technique Tips

Printmaking

Making a Sponge Print

Use a different sponge for each color. Dip a sponge in paint. Press it onto paper.

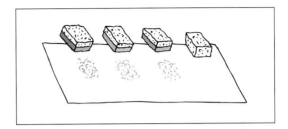

Making a Stencil

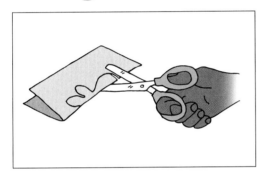

Cut a shape from folded paper.

Sponge Printing with a Stencil

Hold the stencil in place. Press paint into the stencil with a sponge.

Technique Tips
Printmaking
Monoprint

1. Make a design in paint.

2. Lay paper on top. Rub the back.

3. Peel away the paper.

Technique Tips

Transfer Print

1. Fold paper in half. Unfold and draw on one half.

2. Refold the paper and rub.

3. Open the paper.

Technique Tips

Sculpting

Working with Clay

Squeeze, pull, and shape the clay to make it soft. Form clay into an oval shape.

Squeeze and pinch.

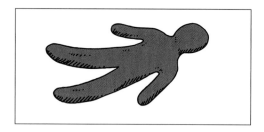

Pinch and pull.

Adding Texture to Clay

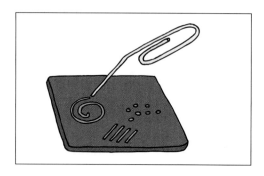

Carve the clay. Use a pointed tool.

Press an object that has texture into the clay.

Technique Tips

Sculpting
Joining Clay

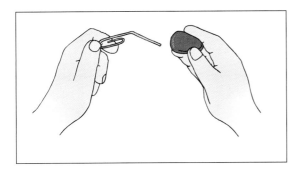

Score the edge.

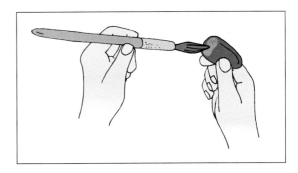

Apply slip.

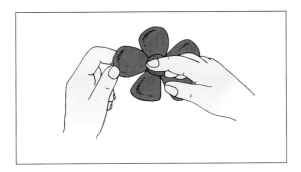

Squeeze and smooth.

Stitchery
The Running Stitch

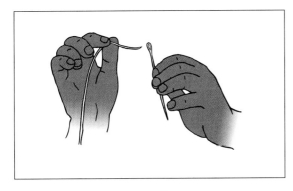

Thread a needle.

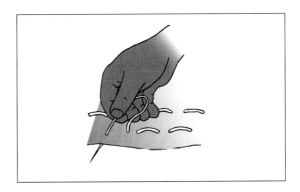

Use a running stitch.

Activity Tips

Line

 Creative Expression

1. Think about thick and thin lines.
2. Create a blanket for yourself with different lines.

. . . .

Lines Can Make Calm Pictures

 Creative Expression

1. Tear the paper into short and long pieces.
2. Place the pieces on the page to make a calm landscape.
3. Glue the pieces to the page.

Activity Tips

Unit 1 · Lesson 3 **Lines Can Make Busy Pictures**

 Creative Expression

1. Use the shape and pencil tools to draw a clown.

2. Make the hair by drawing zigzag lines.

3. Decorate the costume with diagonal lines.

Unit 1 · Lesson 4 **Curved Lines**

 Creative Expression

1. Think of your favorite game to play on the playground.

2. Draw a picture of yourself playing.

3. Use curved and diagonal lines to show things moving.

Activity Tips

Smooth and Rough Lines

 Creative Expression

1. Think about different types of pets.
2. Draw a pet using smooth and rough lines.

- -

Broken Lines

 Creative Expression

1. Cut paper strips into small squares.
2. Glue them to the paper to form an outline of an animal.

Activity Tips

Shape

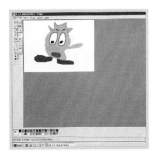

 **Creative Expression**

1. Think about the different imaginary creatures you have seen in books.

2. Draw an imaginary creature of your own.

Geometric Shapes

 **Creative Expression**

1. Cut out some shapes.

2. Choose the ones you like best and glue them on the paper.

Activity Tips

Free-Form Shapes

 Creative Expression

1. Roll ink onto leaves.
2. Press the leaves on your paper.

More About Shapes

 Creative Expression

1. Draw a picture of your house. Use geometric shapes.
2. Draw the background with free-form shapes from nature.

Activity Tips

Body Shapes

 **Creative Expression**

1. Draw a big picture of yourself. Fill the entire sheet of paper.

2. Show how you look today. Draw the clothes you are wearing.

The Shape of People

 Creative Expression

1. Think about the size of people in your family.

2. Cut out different-size shapes to show the people in your family.

3. Arrange the shapes on your paper.

Activity Tips

A Garden of Colors

 Creative Expression

1. Think about the types of flowers you like best.

2. Draw your own flower garden.

Recognizing Objects by Color

 Creative Expression

1. Choose paper that matches the fruit colors.

2. Cut shapes and make a collage.

Activity Tips

Looking at Colors

 **Creative Expression**

1. Create a collage using the color your teacher gives you.

2. Find that color in magazine pictures. Cut out pieces of that color to make your collage.

Primary Colors

 **Creative Expression**

1. Find an object you like.

2. Use red, yellow, and blue markers only. Draw and color a picture of your object.

Activity Tips

Colors Show Feelings

 Creative Expression

1. Choose bright or dull colors for your portrait.
2. Draw your face and body. Then add details.

· ·

Light and Dark Colors

 Creative Expression

1. Create a sea picture with light and dark colors.
2. Add details like fish, waves, and plants.

Activity Tips

Space in Art

 Creative Expression

1. Draw a landscape with trees or houses.
2. Color the sky.

Form

 Creative Expression

1. Make a clay form of yourself.
2. Use a pencil to add a face and clothing.

Activity Tips

Space and Form

 **Creative Expression**

1. Practice holding and moving your paper-towel tube.

2. Use the tube to make a puppet.

A Building Is a Form

 Creative Expression

1. Fill the paper bag with newspaper. Staple a folded piece of paper to the top so it looks like a roof.

2. Decorate your house with doors and windows.

Activity Tips

An Animal Is a Form

 Creative Expression

1. Make an animal with four legs out of clay.
2. Use a pencil to add eyes and other details.

Forms Can Be Used

 Creative Expression

1. Pinch your clay ball to form a pot.
2. Use a pencil to make a design on your pot.

Activity Tips

Texture You Can Touch

 **Creative Expression**

1. Think about the shapes you see in a landscape.

2. Cut out the shapes.

3. Use the shapes to make a landscape with textures.

Texture You Can See

 **Creative Expression**

1. Design a hat that has different textures.

2. Make crayon rubbings to create different textures.

Activity Tips

Designing with Texture

 **Creative Expression**

1. Think about a puppet you would like to make.
2. Choose textured materials for your puppet.
3. Glue the materials on your paper bag.

Fiber Textures

 **Creative Expression**

1. Choose a fiber.
2. Weave the fiber through the slits in the cup.

Activity Tips

Real Texture on Forms

 **Creative Expression**

1. Roll a ball of clay, and then flatten it.
2. Shape the clay into a circle, square, or rectangle.
3. Press objects into the clay to create texture.

Texture on Shapes

 Creative Expression

1. Think of some shapes you could sew.
2. Draw the shapes on your piece of burlap.
3. Sew along the outlines of your shapes.

Activity Tips

Pattern

 Creative Expression

1. Draw a picture of your home.
2. Add patterns to your home.

Rhythm and Movement

 Creative Expression

1. Draw train tracks on your paper.
2. Draw a train on your tracks.

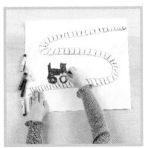

Activity Tips

Balance

 **Creative Expression**

1. Fold your paper in half the long way.
2. Cut shapes into the unfolded edge.

- -

Balance in Sculpture

 Creative Expression

1. Cut shapes for the face, arms, and legs of the creature.
2. Glue them to the tube so they are balanced.

Activity Tips

Unity

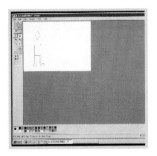

 **Creative Expression**

1. Use the shape tool and line tool to show couples dancing.

2. Draw clothes and other details on your picture.

Unity in Sculpture

 **Creative Expression**

1. Use cardboard tubes to make an animal sculpture.

2. Arrange your sculpture with your classmates' sculptures to make one work of art.

Visual Index

Artist Unknown
Painted Storage Jar
c. 2500–1700 B.C.
(page 146)

Artist Unknown
*Ancient Egyptian Hippo
"William"*
1991–1786 B.C. (page 143)

Artist Unknown
Ritual Wine Container
13th century B.C. (page 173)

Artist Unknown
Ritual Bell
12th century B.C.
(page 198)

Artist Unknown
Camillus
A.D. 41–54. (page 131)

Artist Unknown
*Four Ladies of the Court
Playing Polo*
618–906. (page 207)

Artist Unknown
*Bactrian Camel with
Packsaddle*
700–750. (page 142)

Artist Unknown
Taj Mahal
1638–1648. (page 139)

Jean-Étienne Liotard
*Portrait of Marthe
Marie Tronchin*
c. 1758–1761.
(page 161)

Katsushika Hokusai
Boy Juggling Shells
c. 19th century.
(page 49)

Artist Unknown
House Post
19th century.
(page 199)

Artist Unknown
Fish, Gold Weight
19th–20th century. (page 172)

Artist Unknown
Bowl
c. 1800. (page 147)

William Blake
The Fly from *Songs of Innocence and Experience*
c. 1825. (page 48)

Katsushika Hokusai
The Great Wave Off Kanagawa
1831–1833. (page 34)

Katsushika Hokusai
Kirifuri Waterfall on Mt. Kurokami in Shimotsuke Province
c. 1832–1834.
(page 117)

Currier and Ives
American Express Train
1864. (page 191)

Currier and Ives
My Little White Kittens into Mischief
1865. (page 53)

Artist Unknown
Gift Basket
c. 1870–1880. (page 169)

Artist Unknown
*Classic Serape Style
Wearing Blanket*
1875. (page 36)

W. H. Brown
Bareback Riders
1886. (page 44)

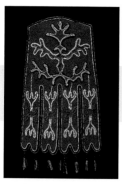

Artist Unknown
Octopus Bag
c. 1890. (page 109)

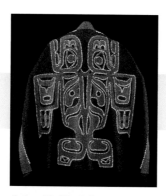

John Yeiltatzie
*Button Robe—Orca
Whale Design*
c. 1890. (page 195)

Louis H. Sullivan
Wainwright Building
1890–1891. (page 187)

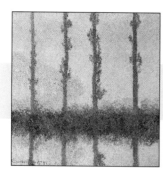

Claude Monet
The Four Trees
1891. (page 40)

John Henry Twachtman
Waterfall Blue Brook
c. 1895–1900.
(page 116)

Harriet Powers
*Bible Quilt, Detail:
Dark Day of May 19, 1780*
c. 1897. (page 176)

Artist Unknown
Hand Puppets
late 19th century.
(page 164)

Artist Unknown
Victorian House
late 19th century.
(page 186)

Felipa Trujillo
Man
early 20th century.
(page 130)

Artist Unknown
Embroidered Pillow
20th century. (page 177)

Maria Martinez
Two Black-on-Black Pots
20th century. (page 184)

Pablo Picasso
The Tragedy
1903. (page 113)

Raoul Dufy
Le Pantheon et Saint-Étienne-du-Mont
c. 1903–1906.
(page 126)

Louis Comfort Tiffany
Garden Landscape and Fountain
c. 1905–1915. (page 56)

A. Schoenhut Co.
American Toymakers
Schoenhut's Humpty Dumpty Circus
c. 1905–1935. (page 45)

Henri-Charles Manguin
Port Saint Tropez, le 14 Juillet
1905. (page 60)

Frank Lloyd Wright
Stockman House
1908. (page 138)

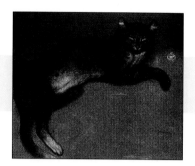

Theophile-Alexandre Steinlen
*L'Hiver, Chat sur un Coussin
(Winter: Cat on a Cushion)*
1909. (page 52)

Marc Chagall
I and the Village
1911. (page 105)

Gabriele Münter
Child with Ball
c. 1916. (page 160)

Georgia O'Keeffe
*Autumn Leaves,
Lake George, N.Y.*
1924. (page 75)

Edward Hopper
The Lighthouse at Two Lights
1929. (page 127)

Grant Wood
American Gothic
1930. (page 64)

Artist Unknown
Conchero Pull Toys
1930s. (page 165)

Diego Rivera
Zandunga Tehuantepec Dance
c. 1935. (page 202)

Allan Rohan Crite
School's Out
1936. (page 78)

Henri Matisse
Woman in a Purple Coat
1937. (page 94)

Edouard Vuillard
Morning in the Garden at Vaucresson
1937. (page 97)

Henri Matisse
La Musique (Music)
1939. (page 108)

Joseph Stella
The Brooklyn Bridge: Variations on an Old Theme
1939. (page 210)

Henry Moore
Reclining Figure
1939. (page 134)

Jacob Lawrence
Harriet Tubman Series #4
1939–1940. (page 83)

William H. Johnson
Li'l Sis
1944. (page 82)

Ben Shahn
World's Greatest Comics
1946. (page 79)

Artist Unknown
Butterfly
c. 1950. (page 194)

Auguste Herbin
Composition on the Word "Vie" 2
1950. (page 70)

Jacob Lawrence
Still Life with Grapes and Roses
1954. (page 101)

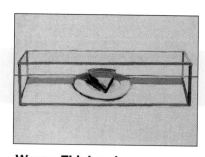

Wayne Thiebaud
Caged Pie
1962. (page 71)

Maurice Sendak
Where the Wild Things Are
1963. (page 66)

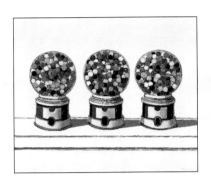

Wayne Thiebaud
Three Machines
1963. (page 104)

George Segal
The Diner
1964–1966. (page 150)

David Hockney
American Collectors
1968. (page 41)

Mercer Mayer
*There's a Nightmare
in My Closet*
1976. (page 67)

Jack Savitsky
Train in Coal Town
1968. (page 190)

Marc Chagall
The Four Seasons
1974. (page 57)

Allan Houser
Earth Song
1978. (page 124)

Betty Parsons
Winged Frog
1978. (page 156)

Audrey Flack
Energy Apples
1980. (page 100)

Rodney Alan Greenblat
Control Chair
1986. (page 120)

John Hoover
Eagle and Salmon
1987. (page 157)

Artist Unknown
Appalachian Basket
1988. (page 168)

Romare Bearden
Family
1988. (page 87)

Janet Fish
Feeding Caitlin
1988. (page 112)

David Wiesner
Free Fall
1988. (page 74)

Sandy Skoglund
The Green House
1990. (page 206)

Sylvia Long
Illustration from *Ten Little Rabbits*
1991. (page 37)

Leo Twiggs
Big Blues Man II
1993. (page 90)

Peggy Flora Zalucha
Sprinkler Garden
1994. (page 96)

Duane Hanson
Old Couple on a Bench
1994–1995. (page 135)

Carmen Lomas Garza
Dance at El Jardin
1996. (page 203)

Miriam Schapiro
Father and Daughter
1997. (page 86)

Peggy Flora Zalucha
My Dad's Violin
1998. (page 180)

Beau Dick
*Urban Raven/Urban Indian
Transformation Mask*
2002. (page 154)

Glossary

art form
A type of art

black

blue

bright colors

broken line

brown

circle

collage
Bits and pieces of things glued onto paper

color

curved lines

darker

diagonal line

dull colors

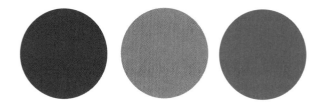

even balance

Both halves are equal. Left side and right side are the same.

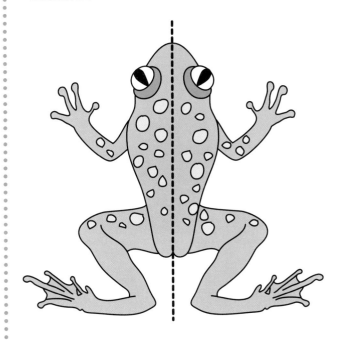

fiber

A material used to make baskets and cloth. Grass, yarn, and straw are kinds of fibers.

form

free-form shapes

geometric shapes

green

horizontal lines

lighter

Mixing a color with white makes it lighter.

line

movement

mural

A painting done on a wall

orange

outline

painting

An art form using paint on a flat surface

pattern

primary colors
Red, yellow, and blue

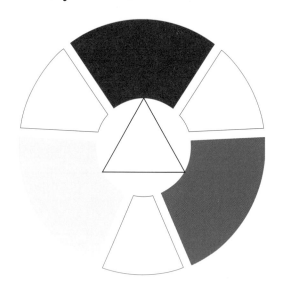

printing
Pressing a shape from one thing to another many times

real texture
Texture you can feel

rectangle

red

rough line

rhythm

sculpture
A kind of art that can be seen from all sides

shape

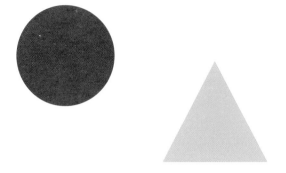

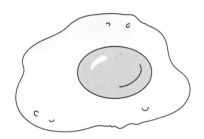

smooth line

space
The empty places around and between shapes.

square

stitchery
Art made with yarn on cloth

texture
How something feels

thick line

thin line

triangle

unity

A feeling of belonging together

vertical lines

violet

visual texture

Texture you can see, but cannot touch

white

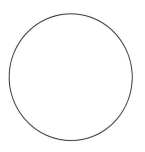

yellow

zigzag line

Index

Acknowledgments Grateful acknowledgment is given to the following publishers and copyright owners for permissions granted to reprint selections from their publications. All possible care has been taken to trace ownership and secure permission for each selection included. In case of any errors or omissions, the publisher will be pleased to make suitable acknowledgments in future editions.

From TEN LITTLE RABBITS © 1991 by Virginia Grossman, illustrated by Sylvia Long. Used with permission of Chronicle Books LLC, San Francisco. Visit ChronicleBooks.com.

From THERE'S A NIGHTMARE IN MY CLOSET by Mercer Mayer, copyright © 1968 by Mercer Mayer. Used by permission of Dial Books for Young Readers, A Division of Penguin Young Readers Group, A Member of Penguin Group (USA) Inc., 345 Hudson Street, New York, NY 10014. All rights reserved.

WHERE THE WILD THINGS ARE

FREE FALL

Photo Credits 12 (tl) Columbus Museum of Art, Ohio: Museum Purchase, Howard Fund II. ©The Georgia O'Keeffe Foundation/Arts Rights Society (ARS) , New York, (bl) The Metropolitan Museum of Art, Gift of Henry G. Marquand, 1897. (97.22.25) Photograph ©2000 The Metropolitan Museum of Art, (br) ©Corbis; 13 (br) Buffalo Bill Historical Center, Cody WY Chandler-Pohrt Collection, Gift of The Searle Family Trust and The Paul Stock Foundation; 13 (tr) Smithsonian American Art Museum, Washington, DC. Gift of Catherine McIntosh / Art Resource, NY, (tl) Honolulu Academy of Arts, Honolulu, Hawaii. Gift of James A. Michener, 1976 (16,794); 14 ©2004 Board of Trustees, National Gallery of Art, Washington, DC. Gift of Edgar William and Bernice Chrysler Garbisch; 15 Georgia Museum of Art - University of Georgia - Athens - Georgia. Eva Underhill Holbrook Memorial Collection of American Art. Gift of Alfred H. Holbrook; 16 The Sidney and Harriet Janis Collection (606.1967) Digital Image ©The Museum of Modern Art/Licensed by SCALA/Art Resource, NY. ©2004 Artist Rights Society (ARS) , New York/ADAGP, Paris; 17 The Metropolitan Museum of Art, H.O. Havemeyer Collection, Bequest of Mrs. H.O. Havemeyer, 1929. Photography ©1996 The Metropolitan Museum of Art; 21 (t) International Folk Art Foundation Collection. Museum of International Folk Art. Santa Fe, New Mexico. Photo by: Pat Pollard, (b) The Roland P. Murdock Collection, Wichita Art Museum, Wichita, Kansas; 24, 26, 28 Museum of Fine Arts, Houston, Texas. The John A. and Audrey Jones Beck Collection; 34 The Metropolitan Museum of Art, H.O. Havemeyer Collection, Bequest of Mrs. H.O. Havemeyer, 1929. (JP1847) Photograph ©1994 The Metropolitan Museum of Art,; 35 ©Getty Images; 37 Chronicle Books; 40 The Metropolitan Museum of Art, H.O. Havemeyer Collection, Bequest of Mrs. H.O. Havemeyer, 1929. Photography ©1996 The Metropolitan Museum of Art; 41 Restricted gift of Mr. and Mrs. Frederic G. Pick, 1984.182. Photograph ©2002, The Art Institute of Chicago, All Rights Reserved; 43 Randy Ellett; 44 ©2004 Board of Trustees, National Gallery of Art, Washington, DC. Gift of Edgar William and Bernice Chrysler Garbisch; 45 ©Children's Museum of Indianapolis; 47 Randy Ellett; 48 The Metropolitan Museum of Art, Rogers Fund, 1917; 49 The Metropolitan Museum of Art, New York, New York. Charles Stewart Smith Collection. Gift of Mrs. Charles Stewart Smith, in memory of Charles Stewart Smith, 1914; 52 The Metropolitan Museum of Art, The Elisha Whittelsey Collection, The Elisha Whittelsey Fund, 1950; 53 The Metropolitan Museum of Art, Bequest of Adele S. Colgate, 1963, (63.550.479) Photograph © 1981 The Metropolitan Museum of Art; 55 Randy Ellett; 56 The Metropolitan Museum of Art, Gift of Lillian Nassau, 1976, and Gift of Mrs. L. Groves Geer, 1978. (1976.105, 1978.584) Photograph © 1998 The Metropolitan Museum of Art; 56 The Metropolitan Museum of Art, Gift of Lillian Nassau, 1976, and Gift of Mrs. L. Groves Geer, 1978. (1976.105, 1978.584) Photograph © 1998 The Metropolitan Museum of Art; 57 Photo ©Mary Ann Sullivan. ©2004 Artist Rights Society (ARS) , New York/ADAGP, Paris; 60 The Bridgeman Art Library; 61 Photo courtesy of The Museum of Fine Arts, Houston, Texas; 62 Vic Luke; 63 The Museum of Modern Art, New York, New York. Acquired through the Lille P. Bliss Bequest. Photograph ©2004 The Museum of Modern Art, New York; 64 The Art Institute of Chicago. ©2004 Estate of Grant Wood/Licensed by VAGA, New York, New York; 65 Courtesy of the Curtis Galleries - Inc. - Minneapolis - MN. ©1998 Estate of Grant Wood/Licensed by VAGA - New York - NY; 66 Harper and Row Publishers; 67 Dial Books for Young Readers; 69 Randy Ellett; 70 The Sidney and Harriet Janis Collection (606.1967) Digital Image ©The Museum of Modern Art/Licensed by SCALA/Art Resource, NY. ©2004 Artist Rights Society (ARS) , New York/ADAGP, Paris; 71 © Wayne Thiebaud/Licensed by VAGA, New York, New York; 72 ©Eclipse Studios; 74 Courtesy of Lothrop, Lee, and Shepard Books; 75 Columbus Museum of Art, Ohio: Museum Purchase, Howard Fund II. ©The Georgia O'Keeffe Foundation/Arts Rights Society (ARS) , New York; 78 Smithsonian American Art Museum, Washington, DC./Art Resource, NY; 79 Amon Carter Museum, Fort Worth, Texas. 1974.24. ©Estate of Ben Shahn/Licensed by VAGA, New York, NY; 81 Randy Ellett; 82 Smithsonian American Art Museum. Washington, DC./Art Resource, NY; 83 Hampton University Art Museum, Hampton, Virginia. ©Jacob and Gwendolyn Lawrence Foundation; 86 ©1997 Miriam Schapiro; 87 ©Smithsonian American Art Museum, Washington, DC/Art Resource, NY. ©Romare Bearden Foundation/Licensed by VAGA, New York, NY; 89 Randy Ellett; 90 ©Leo Twiggs; 92 Photograph courtesy of Jerry Pinkney; 93 Judy Francesconi; 94 The Museum of Fine Arts, Houston; Gift of Audrey Jones Beck. ©2004 Succession H. Matisse, Paris/Artist Rights Society (ARS), New York; 96 Courtesy of Peggy Flora Zaluch; 97 The Metropolitan Museum of Art, Catharine Lorillard Wolfe Collection, Wolfe Fund, 1952. (52.183) ©2004 Artist Rights Society (ARS) New York/ADAGP, Paris. 100 ©Courtesy Louis K. Meisel Gallery, New York; 101 © ARS, NY. © Photograph Courtesy of Gwendolyn Knight Lawrence / Art Resource, NY; 102 (tl) Comstock, (tr) Photodisc/Getty Images, (b)©Eclipse Studios; 103 Randy Ellett; 104 Fine Arts Museum of San Francisco. Museum purchase, Walter H. and Phyllis J. Shorenstein Foundation Fund and the Roscoe and Margaret Oakes Income Fund, with additional gifts from Claire E. Flagg; The Museum Society Auxiliary; Mr. and Mrs. George R. Roberts; Mr. and Mrs. John N. Rosekrans; and from the Morgan Flagg Collection., 1993.18 ©Wayne Thiebaud/Licensed by VAGA, New York, NY; 105 Digital Image©The Museum of Modern Art/Licensed by SCALA/Art Resource, NY. ©2004 Artist Rights Society (ARS) , New York/ADAGP, Paris; 108 Albright-Knox Gallery, Buffalo, New York, Room of Contemporary Art Fund, 1940. ©2004 Succession H. Matisse, Paris/Artist Rights Society (ARS) , New York; 109 Seattle Art Museum. Paul Macapia, photographer; 110 Randy Ellett; 111 Yale University Art Gallery, New Haven Connecticut; 112 Photo Courtesy of Paul Tracey; 112 Museum Purchase, 1999. Butler Institute of American Art, Youngstown, Ohio. ©Janet Fish/Licensed by VAGA, New York, NY; 113 National Gallery of Art, Washington D.C. Chester Dale Collection. ©2004 Estate of Pablo Picasso/Artist Rights Society (ARS) , New York; 114 (tr, bl, br) PhotoDisc/Getty Images, Inc, (tr) Digital Vision; 115 Randy Ellett; 116 Cincinnati Art Museum, Annual Membership Fund 1900.44; 117 Honolulu Academy of Arts, Honolulu, Hawaii. Gift of James A. Michener, 1976 (16,794) ; 119 Randy Ellett; 126 Albright-Knox Art Gallery. By exchange, George B. and Jenny R. Mathews and a Bequest of A. Conger Goodyear and Gift of Colonel Charles Clifton, 1980. ©2004 Artist Rights Society (ARS) New York/ADAGP, Paris; 127 The Metropolitan Museum of Art, Hugo Kastor Fund, 1962. (62.95) Photograph © 1990 The Metropolitan Museum of Art; 128 Photodisc/Getty Images, Inc; 129 Randy Ellett; 130 From the Girard Foundation Collection, in the Museum of International Folk Art, a unit of the Museum of New Mexico, Sante Fe, New Mexico. Photographer: Michel Monteaux; 131 The Metropolitan Museum of Art, Gift of Henry G. Marquand, 1897. (97.22.25) Photograph ©2000 The Metropolitan Museum of Art; 132 ©Matt Meadows; 133 Randy Ellett; 134 Founders Society Purchase with funds from the Dexter M. Ferry, Jr. Trustee Corporation. Photograph © 1985 The Detroit Institute of Arts; 135 Courtesy of Mrs. Duane Henson. Art © Estate of Duane Hanson/Licensed by VAGA, New York, NY; 136 (t) Photodisc/Getty Images, Inc, (b) ©Eclipse Studios; 137 Randy Ellett; 138 ©Don Gunning; 139 ©Corbis; 141 Randy Ellett; 142 The Nelson Atkins Museum, Kansas City, Missouri. (Purchase: acquired through the Joyce C. Hall Funds of the Community Foundation, the Joyce C. Hall Estate, The Donald J. Hall Designated Fund of the Community Foundation, the Barbara Hall Marshall Designated Fund, and the Elizabeth Ann Reid Donor Advisory fund) F83-8/3. Photograph by E.G. Schempf; 143 The Metropolitan Museum of Art, New York, New York. Gift of Edward S. Harkness, 1917; 144 ©Eclipse Studios; 145 Roz Ragans; 147 Founders Society Purchase, with funds from Richard A. Manoogian, the new Endowment Fund, the Joseph H. Boyer Memorial Fund and the Mr. and Mrs. Walter B. Ford II Fund. Photograph © 1991 The Detroit Institute of Arts; 148 (tl) Photodisc/Getty Images, Inc, (tr) Gourmet Sleuth.Com, (b) Corel; 150 Collection Walker Art Center, Minneapolis. Gift of T.B. Walker Foundation, 1966; 152 (r) Tom Wagner/Corbis, (br) Courtesy of Nelson-Atkins Museum, Kansas City, Missouri; 153 Craig Schwartz Photography ©1992; 155 Douglas Reynolds Gallery, Vancouver, British Columbia, Canada; 156 The National Museum of Women in the Arts, Washington, DC. Gift of Wallace and Wilhelmina Holladay; 157 Photograph by Steve Cox; 159 Randy Ellett; 160 The National Museum of Women in the Arts, Washington, DC. On loan from the Wallace and Wilhelmina Holladay Collection. ©2004 Artist Rights Society (ARS) , New York/VG Bild Kunst, Bonn; 161 Clarence Buckingham Collection, 1985.252. Photograph ©2000, The Art Institute of Chicago, All Rights Reserved; 163 Randy Ellett; 164 From the Girard Foundation Collection, in the Museum of International Folk Art, a unit of the Museum of New Mexico, Santa Fe, New Mexico. Photographer: Michel Monteaux; 165 San Antonio Museum of Art; 166 ©Eclipse Studios; 167 Randy Ellett; 168 Frank Fortune; 169 The Lowe Art Museum, The University of Miami, Coral Gables, Florida. Donated by Alfred I. Barton; 170 (l) Photodisc/Getty Images, Inc, (c) ©Paul Rocheleau/Index Stock Imagery, r) ©Leslie Harris/Index Stock; 172 The Metropolitan Museum of Art, The Michael C. Rockefeller Memorial Collection, Gift of Nelson A, Rockefeller, 1969 (1978.412.567) Photograph ©1996 The Metropolitan Museum of Art; 173 Arthur M. Sackler Gallery, Smithsonian Institution, Washington, D.C.: Gift of Arthur M. Sackler; 175, 179 Randy Ellett; 180 ©Peggy Flora Zalucha; 184 Courtesy of Maria Martinez; 185 Courtesy Maria Martinez ©Jerry Jacka Photography; 186 ©Doug Keister; 187 ©Art on File/Corbis; 189 Randy Ellett; 190 Smithsonian American Art Museum, Washington, DC./Art Resource, NY; 191 ©Scala/Art Resource, NY; 193 Randy Ellett; 194 From the Girard Foundation Collection, in the Museum of International Folk Art, a unit of the Museum of New Mexico, Santa Fe, New Mexico. Photographer: Michel Monteaux; 195 Seattle Art Museum. Paul Macapia, photographer; 197 Randy Ellett; 198 Arthur M. Sackler Gallery, Smithsonian Institution, Washington, DC.: Gift of Arthur M. Sackler, S1987.10; 199 The Brooklyn Museum of Art. Museum Expedition 1911, Museum Collection Fund 11.700.1; 200 (l) Photodisc/Getty Images, Inc, (r) Corel; 201 Randy Ellett; 202 Los Angeles County Museum of Art, Gift of Mr. and Mrs. Milton W. Lipper; 204 (t) Photodisc/Getty Images, Inc, (b) ©Eclipse Studios; 205 Randy Ellett; 206 THE GREEN HOUSE ©1990 Sandy Skoglund; 207 The Nelson-Atkins Museum of Art, Kansas City, Missouri (Purchase: acquired through the generosity of Katherine Harvey); 208 (l) ©Bridgeman Art Library, (r) Photodisc/Getty Images, Inc; 209 Randy Ellett; 210 Purchase, Whitney Museum of American Art, New York. Photo by Geoffrey Clements; 211 (t) Photodisc/Getty Images, Inc, (b) Eclipse Studios; 212 ©Getty Images Inc; 213 Craig Schwartz Photography ©1998; 232 ©Eclipse Studios; 233 (t) Aaron Haupt, (b) Matt Meadows; 234 ©Eclipse Studios; 235 (t) Aaron Haupt, (b) Matt Meadows; 236 (t) ©Eclipse Studios, (b) Aaron Haupt; 237 (t) Aaron Haupt, (b) ©Eclipse Studios; 238 (t) ©Eclipse Studios, (b) Aaron Haupt; 239 (t) ©Eclipse Studios, (b) Aaron Haupt; 240 ©Eclipse Studios; 241 (t) ©Eclipse Studios, (b) Aaron Haupt; 242 ©Eclipse Studios; 243 Aaron Haupt; 244 (t) Aaron Haupt, (b) ©Eclipse Studios; 245, 246 Aaron Haupt; 247, 248 ©Eclipse Studios; 249 (t) Matt Meadows, (b) ©Eclipse Studios.